Quality and regulation in health care

Quality and regulation in health care
International experiences

Edited by Robert Dingwall and Paul Fenn

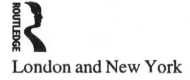

London and New York

First published in 1992
by Routledge
11 New Fetter Lane, London EC4P 4EE

Simultaneously published in the USA and Canada
by Routledge
a division of Routledge, Chapman and Hall Inc.
29 West 35th Street, New York, NY 10001

Typeset in Times by LaserScript, Mitcham, Surrey
Printed and bound in Great Britain by
Mackays of Chatham PLC, Chatham, Kent

British Library Cataloguing in Publication Data
A catalogue record for this book is available from the British Library.

Library of Congress Cataloging in Publication Data
Quality and regulation in health care: international experiences/ edited by
    Robert Dingwall and Paul Fenn.
        p.   cm.
    Includes bibliographical references and index.
    1. Medical care–Quality control.   2. Medical care–Law and legislation.
    I. Dingwall, Robert.   II. Fenn, Paul. [DNLM: 1. Delivery of Health
    Care–congresses.   2. Delivery of Health Care–legislation.   3. Quality of
    Health Care–congresses.   4. Quality of Health Care–legislation. W 84.1 Q13]
    RA399.A1Q28   1992
    362.1'068'5–dc20
    DNLM/DLC
for Library of Congress   92–3926
                                                                             CIP
    ISBN 0–415–05503–2

92   00924

Contents

Tables

Contributors

Robert Dingwall Professor of Social Studies, University of Nottingham.

Paul Fenn Research Fellow, Wolfson College and Centre for Socio-Legal Studies, University of Oxford.

Stephen Daniels Research Fellow, American Bar Foundation, Chicago.

David Hughes Lecturer, School of Social Studies, University of Nottingham.

Timothy Jost Professor of Law, Ohio State University, Columbus, Ohio.

Sally Lloyd-Bostock Research Fellow, Wolfson College and Centre for Socio-Legal Studies, University of Oxford.

Alistair McGuire Research Fellow, Pembroke College and Centre for Socio-Legal Studies, University of Oxford.

Linda Mulcahy Research Officer, Centre for Socio-Legal Studies, University of Oxford.

Marilynn M. Rosenthal Professor and Director of the Health and Society Program, University of Michigan-Dearborn.

Introduction

Robert Dingwall and Paul Fenn

Throughout the Western world, health care systems are grappling with the problem of assuring quality while containing costs. On the one hand, governments and insurers argue that there must be some limit to the apparently endless growth of health care expenditures. On the other hand, patient groups and consumer advocates, already dissatisfied as a result of the problems in holding doctors accountable for their actions, assert that such limits must not prevent patients from gaining access to essential treatments. The two movements find common cause in the development of systems of regulation intended to police the quality of care. Some of these are initiated by individuals, like the tort system of litigation over particular acts of negligence or the work of licensing boards reacting to complaints about a physician's fitness to practise. Others are corporate, as in the spread of medical audit or the introduction of schemes of managerial control. Such regulatory systems, it is believed, can combine the prevention of ineffective, dangerous or inefficient medical practices with the promotion of high technical standards of care and sensitivity to consumer demands or expectations.

The regulation of social institutions, whether by legal or extra-legal means, has long been a central concern for socio-legal studies. Until recently, however, that body of work has found little application in studies of the delivery of health care. At the same time, studies in medical sociology and health economics have taken scant account of the legal framework which surrounds the provision of health services in all advanced societies. Even the most obvious exception, the corpus of research on medical negligence litigation in the United States, has produced a literature insulated from sociological and economic thinking about health care organizations and the perspectives of socio-legal studies on dispute processing.

This volume arose out of the contributors' desire to broaden the framework within which the regulation of quality in health care was analysed. It has developed from papers presented in a session at the 1989 meetings of the Law and Society Association in Madison, WI, and revised across two continents and numerous *ad hoc* conversations.

Our analysis begins with the editors' discussion of the tort system, the oldest means by which people have tried to hold medical practitioners accountable for their actions and to enforce the provision of a reasonable quality of care. Characteristically, the earliest recorded cases also show the difficulties faced by dissatisfied patients in using this method of seeking redress. In *The Surgeon's Case* of 1375, the plaintiff failed because the writ had been improperly drafted, while in 1423 another surgeon was exonerated, in *Forest v Harowe*, because a special jury, including physicians, decided that the mishap involved was due either to some failure on the patient's part or to the nature of the original wound or to the phase of the moon (Jacob and Davies 1987: 1–33). Nevertheless, by 1470–71, Choke, J. could declare as an established doctrine: 'If a man undertakes to cure me of a certain disease, and he gives me medicine which makes me worse, I shall have action against him' (quoted in Holdsworth 1942: VIII: 387). Anybody who represented themselves as a healer and caused harm to a patient, by failing to practise their art to the standard expected by a lay jury and other recognized practitioners, was liable to compensate the victim.

The fundamental principles of tort liability for negligence or malpractice and their justifications have changed little since that time. Actions for tort rest on the assumption that all members of a society owe each other a duty of care to avoid harming each other, whether the injury is to the person or his or her legitimate interests. If someone fails in this duty, he or she should pay compensation to the victim sufficient to restore him, so far as possible, to his previous condition. The risk of such a payment constitutes an incentive for potential wrongdoers to take their duty of care seriously and to make such investments as are appropriate to reduce the likelihood of harm being caused.

In the particular case of the medical profession, negligence is a breach of a doctor's duty to use reasonable care in his or her treatment of a patient which results in an injury to that patient. For a tort action to succeed, the patient will have to show both a causal relationship between the doctor's action, or inaction, and the injury and that the doctor's conduct deviated from the profession's customary standard of care. The standard of care is determined by the court in the light of expert evidence given by fellow-members of the medical profession. The questions are exactly those put before the special jury in *Forest v Harowe*, over five hundred years ago. Was there a causal relationship between the surgeon's intervention and the patient's condition or was it due to some exogenous influence like the moon? Had the surgeon used an appropriate technique and been defeated by the nature of the original injury? Was the adverse outcome to be attributed to the surgeon or had the plaintiff failed to comply with properly prescribed medical treatment?

Much of the discussion about the relevance of the tort system to the practice of medicine has focused upon its inadequacies as a system of compensation. The questions posed in *Forest v Harowe* are no easier to answer in the twentieth century than in the fifteenth. As a result, there are many well-recognized inequities in the outcome of tort actions. Like needs receive unlike compensation. 'Deserving' cases fail on the uncertainties of causation. Doctors who commit egregious errors are spared public humiliation by negotiated settlements while others who made an unlucky judgement in a finely balanced situation find their careers blighted by lurid trial reports in the tabloid press. Uncertainties over the outcome inhibit settlement negotiations, prolonging cases and driving up costs. There is a substantial literature on the attempts to develop alternatives to tort, whether by means of social security, *ad hoc* no-fault compensation schemes or private insurance (Dingwall *et al.* 1991).

However, the tort action may have other functions in addition to compensation. First, it can offer an element of non-financial compensation to the plaintiff in the psychological satisfaction of obtaining some form of retribution from the public exposure of the wrongdoer. In the United States, this may be compounded by a levy of punitive damages, to penalize the defendant over and above what is necessary to make good the victim's losses, although these are uncommon in medical cases (Daniels and Martin 1990).[1] Second, it can be a means of obtaining a public inquiry into the causes of a mishap through the opportunity to examine witnesses and obtain a judicial declaration of the chain of events linked to the occurrence of injury and the allocation of responsibility among the actors involved. In this respect, tort actions can be a general source of information to the community as a whole about the management of risks.

Finally, negligence litigation is seen by many lawyers, and some patient advocates, as a significant incentive for individual health care providers to adopt safe working practices and to follow the highest standards of care, as declared by experts in the course of their evidence. The analysis reviews the difficulties in using information on medical negligence claims for risk management purposes when that information is collected in a decentralized manner. It is argued that, in those circumstances, the tort system is characterized by random, weak and diffuse signals which give little or no worthwhile guidance to individuals or institutions about quality investment. It is only when data are collected at the most aggregate levels that the signals become any clearer, although difficulties remain in relation to the identification of events considered to be 'failures' in medical practice. However, the editors present evidence from a cross-national comparison which does help to identify some clear differences in the costs associated with each system, as represented by legal expenses and the payment of damages. It also points up some additional areas which might repay further investigation, such as the apparent tendency of US physicians to encounter a high rate of claims relating to diagnosis rather than treatment, although it is not clear whether this represents a real difference or whether it is because of different conventions in the drafting of claims by US and UK lawyers. While expressing caution against over-inflated expectations of what the tort system can deliver by means of quality information, the editors argue that some of their results point in directions that might lead to a more constructive approach to outcome-based quality control in the health sector.

The editors' contribution therefore focuses on the empirical basis for the role of the tort system as a means of generating information about the quality of care. It asks whether such information can help to influence decisions about desirable investments by professionals and organizations in the reduction of risk, through greater attention to safety, additional training and skill development or changes in the physical plant and technology for service delivery.

The other traditional means of quality control in health care has been the operation of professional licensing regimes. In England, for example, the first regulatory legislation appeared in 'An Acte concernynge the approbation of physicyons and surgions' in 1512. The Act's preamble declared

> the science and cunning of physic and surgery . . . is daily within this realm exercised by a great multitude of ignorant persons . . . [who] boldly and accustomably have taken upon themselves great cures, and things of great difficulty, in which they partly use sorcery and witchcraft, partly apply such medicines unto the disease as to be very noious, and nothing meet therefore, to the high displeasure of God great infamy to the faculty and the grievous hurt, damage and destruction of many of the King's liege people.
>
> (3 Henry VIII, c.11)

In order to prevent these evils, healers were to be officially licensed, either by a university or by their local bishop. Anyone who did not have the appropriate permit would be subject to a substantial fine.

Enforcement, it should be said, was patchy: Pelling and Webster (1979) found that the diocese of Norwich did not take up the task on any scale until 1583 and there was no serious harassment of unlicensed practitioners until 1597. The neighbouring diocese of Ely did not try to exclude unlicensed healers until 1638. Presumably, the Tudor church had more pressing problems and higher priorities among the many administrative burdens which it acquired on behalf of the state in the course of the sixteenth century. In

Marilynn Rosenthal's contribution to this volume, she notes that patchiness of enforcement continues to be characteristic of licensing boards in the twentieth century. Their activities are limited by the resources which the state is prepared to invest, or to require the profession to invest, in the form of retention fees. This seems to apply regardless of whether the licensing process is controlled by the state, as in the United States of America and Sweden, or by the profession itself, as in the United Kingdom.

These resource limitations contain disciplinary activity at a low level and direct its focus to those matters which prompt patients to complain, and which raise straightforward issues requiring little further investigation, or to those which are swept in automatically by reports from other agencies, such as convictions for drug-related offences. Doctors appear to be differentially vulnerable to reporting, depending on their specialty and integration with local medical communities. It is only in Sweden, where the licensing board has a majority of consumers, that the maintenance of clinical quality, rather than behavioural propriety, has been a major object of attention. Even there, Rosenthal concludes that the board's impact has been marginal. Although the board has reviewed cases involving a higher proportion of the profession, Sweden has fewer alternative means of pursuing complaints about quality, either through administrative channels or, because of its no-fault compensation scheme, through litigation. Rosenthal implies that the overall level of scrutiny to which the medical profession has been subjected differs little between the three countries which she studied.

In the United Kingdom, patients traditionally have a third route for expressing grievances about the quality of care. This is the administrative system which has been established in the National Health Service to deal with patient complaints. The system has three main components: one relates to Family Health Services Authorities (formerly Family Practitioner Committees) which hold the contracts under which self-employed practitioners in primary care provide medical, dental, optical and pharmaceutical services to NHS patients; a second relates to the work of the Health Services Commissioner, who is empowered to investigate complaints of maladministration by health service providers; and a third which deals with hospital complaints. As Rawlings (1987) has remarked, NHS grievance machinery has been 'a backwater of socio-legal study', although one might make mention of the work of Klein (1973) and Allsop and May (1986) on the management of complaints by Family Practitioner Committees. Their powers and approach are essentially a continuation of the system set up to control providers under the health insurance scheme introduced in 1911. It focuses on the compliance of practitioners with the terms of their contract rather than with the quality of care which has been offered. Unless there has been a breach of contract, the authority has very little scope to intervene.

Linda Mulcahy and Sally Lloyd-Bostock present early findings from their work on hospital complaints, which has been the first major attempt to look at this sector. The Department of Health has long recognized that these have a dual character, with some relating to the 'hotel' aspects of care – food, cleaning, waiting times, etc. – while others deal more directly with clinical matters and have often been thought to be an alternative to litigation. A number of recent authors have argued that complaints represent a free source of quality information. If consumers can be encouraged to complain, managers and clinicians can use the data generated to monitor the service which they are providing and introduce patient-responsive improvements. Indeed, the complaints process can, itself, be turned into an opportunity to promote consumer satisfaction by displaying the service's sensitivity to grievances and its desire to resolve them.

While Mulcahy and Lloyd-Bostock accept that complaints are important to the individuals who make them, they are, however, cautious about taking them at face value. There are many reasons why people may or may not complain which are not randomly distributed in the population. The presenting complaint may mask rather than express the felt grievance. Patients may focus on 'hotel' issues because these fall within anyone's competence to judge – we all know when we have eaten a bad lunch – rather than because they are the focus of their dissatisfaction. They note the limited responses of many managers and clinicians, who tend to react to patient letters at a rather superficial level and to emphasize speed of response rather than thoroughness of investigation and commitment to change. In fairness, speed has become the main performance indicator for complaint managers, especially with the obligation to present quarterly statements of outstanding cases, and, as Mulcahy and Lloyd-Bostock point out, the intrinsic biases of the complainant population may well make a heavy investment of managerial or clinician time inappropriate.

These three chapters, taken together, present a fairly gloomy picture of the capacity of the traditional formal mechanisms for the expression of patient dissatisfaction to make a significant impact on the quality of care. Their effects are too limited, diffuse and random to have a great influence on standards of care or to provide an appropriate direction for the investment of managerial or clinical time or resources in measures to assure quality. The next two contributions examine recent attempts to address this problem by introducing more general changes in the social relations between care providers which are intended to give concerns for quality a higher place on organizational and professional agendas. These systems are intended to be proactive and corporate, so that they avoid the problems of bias inherent in any individually triggered means of seeking redress for poor-quality care.

Timothy Jost reports on a review of medical audit in Western Europe and the United States. He describes how he started from the assumption that decades of public involvement in health care provision would have led European governments to develop methods of quality assurance in advance of those recently established in the United States, as part of its painful progress towards the establishment of a means of providing all citizens with health services at an affordable cost. What he found was a group of countries – Sweden, the Federal Republic of Germany, Belgium and the United Kingdom – which had only recently sought to take quality issues on board and to discuss how they might be reflected in the organizational arrangements through which health care was delivered. On the other hand, they had all independently taken a different route to that dominating the US developments, namely a professionally led approach to peer review focusing on mutual education about common problems rather than an insurer- or government-driven approach based on penalizing individual deficiencies.

The result is much less costly and, Jost suggests, might have more impact on the standard of care provided by the average practitioner, although, as he notes, the experience of other forms of self-regulation does not encourage great confidence in this conclusion. External controls may have an important role to play in ensuring that peer review does not degenerate into the means of reaffirming professional solidarity described by some studies of the process in the United States (e.g. Arluke 1977; Freidson 1975; Bosk 1979). On the other hand, Jost concludes, the US may have been too quick to abandon attempts to achieve professional co-operation in the reconciliation of service quality and financial pressures and to have developed an over-elaborate framework of regulation which places its own burdens on providers and purchasers alike.

This theme is continued by Hughes and McGuire in their dissection of the British Conservative Government's 1990 reforms in the National Health Service. They note the way in which, from its inception, the NHS had struggled to reconcile Ministerial accountability for the cost and quality of the service with professional autonomy in clinical decision-making. The central authorities had very little control over one of the largest and most complex organizations in the world – an employer of labour in Europe on a scale second only to the Soviet Army, in the oft-repeated phrase of the 1980s. Hughes and McGuire trace the growing pressures to strengthen central control and to shift the balance between bureaucratic and professional lines of authority from the 1973 reorganization onwards. The accretion of central power reached its apotheosis in the internal market of *Working for Patients*, the Government's 1989 White Paper and the resulting legislation, the National Health Service and

Community Care Act 1990. Although it creates the illusion of competition or contestability in its split between service providers and service purchasers, the internal market can only function within an elaborate framework of regulations and dispute resolution systems sustained by the discretion of the Secretary of State.

One clear consequence of the new regime is the encroachment of bureaucratic authority on clinical autonomy. Managers will have more resources for influencing and sanctioning physicians' behaviour than they have ever enjoyed. Hughes and McGuire note the lack of any empirical evidence to support the theory that these changes will actually reduce costs to an acceptable level in terms of the quality of NHS care, which will remain an important source of pressure on Ministers. Suppose, for example, the cheapest way of providing paediatric services involved the creation of a dozen large regional centres, which, in many areas of the UK, might involve children and their parents travelling more than a hundred miles for treatment. If purchasers are supposed to be cost-driven, the result would be the decline of features like open family access, which are valued by physicians and patients alike, and a move away from the integration of community, primary care and hospital services that has been the goal of clinicians and planners for more than a generation. Children might recover from minor surgery as quickly, but with greater psychological trauma, an externality not borne by the NHS. Where the child was the victim of a terminal disease with acute phases, like some cancers, the hospital episodes would occur at a remote centre in isolation from parents and local care providers. It is not difficult to imagine the sentimental resistance to such consequences of formal managerial rationality.

If the new NHS has a real-world model, then, as Hughes and Dingwall (1990a) have pointed out, it is more likely to lie in the former command economies of Eastern Europe than in some idealized free market. There seem to be no convincing reasons to suppose that it will not in time come to suffer the same organizational pathologies and management costs. The result of seeking to decrease clinical costs may be that the savings are more than swallowed up by additional expenditures on information-gathering and enforcement necessary to make the market behave in accordance with the politicians' dictates.

Is this collection, then, no more than an exercise in intellectual nihilism, one of those demonstrations that nothing works which make practical men and women despair of academics? The basis of our rejection of that charge lies in the unique work of Steve Daniels, the final contributor to the collection. Daniels has gone beyond any other scholar in the field in his focus on the shop-floor of medical practice. What do notions of quality and error mean in an everyday context? This meticulous ethnography of two specialist units in a major US teaching hospital brings out one feature which must be the starting point for any policy discussion: mistakes happen in health care all the time. In this respect, health services are no different from other organizations, especially those handling complex technologies in an uncertain environment. Some errors, however, are more consequential than others. The problem is that it may be virtually impossible to predict these in advance or even to recognize them as they occur. Error is a definition of medical process which is contingent on the particular concatenation of circumstances around its occurrence. By corollary, quality might be assumed to lie in the eyes of the beholder. Quality for an anaesthetist may be different from quality for a surgeon, who may in turn take a different view from a rehabilitation specialist, a service manager or a nurse. This is to say nothing, of course, of the patient's view. Such disparities in perception reflect the disparities in information about process and outcome in the health sector. Much of what is said in this collection addresses this issue of information asymmetry. How can the professional expertise of the clinicians be reconciled with the preferences of their patients?

The debate about quality and regulation is a debate about the practical interpretation of this question. How are the different goals to be reconciled? This is a question which theorists may debate for ever. In the real world, people must take practical decisions all the time. Daniels' paper begins to identify a method of understanding how and why those decisions are taken, which will enable us to lay them out for public debate. Are these the principles which we would wish to see adopted? If not, are we willing to countenance the investments – material and cultural – that would be required to alter them? Would the result be an organization that people could work in and which was capable of delivering a reasonable level of service?

The answer, of course, is that compromises must always be made. How much quality at what cost? How much regulation at what cost? The defence of compromises may be a less heroic enterprise than the search for Utopia. Without them, however, Goethe's fear 'that the world will be a huge hospital and one will be the humane nurse of the other' may yet come to pass.

NOTE

1 A recent British attempt to argue for punitive damages in a medical case was dismissed by the judge in *Kralj v McGrath*.

1 The tort system and information
Some comparisons between the UK and the US

Paul Fenn and Robert Dingwall

One of the difficulties in evaluating the influence of the tort system on the standards and practices of the medical profession has been the diffuse nature of the information flows generated by negligence claims. Tort actions for medical negligence tend to be brought by single plaintiffs against single defendants or a small group of defendants united on an *ad hoc* basis by their involvement with the care of the individual victim of an adverse event. The overwhelming majority of cases where negligence is admitted are settled privately between the parties and there is no public statement about the outcome. Claim databases, if they exist at all, are the property of insurers and have an obvious commercial value in the determination of premium loadings and risk management investments.

On the other hand, the value to the public of such data is equally clear. To the extent that tort claims signal the presence of sub-standard medical care, information on the frequency and severity of such claims can contribute to the effective monitoring of quality in the health care sector. Given that such data, once collected, could be disseminated at very low cost, it seems that it is socially beneficial for private databases to be made public. However, this misses the point that the information would not be collected by insurers if it were to be made public, as it would no longer lead to any private return.

This is the essence of a dilemma which is at the heart of the economics of information: how is it possible to give appropriate incentives for *producing* information without at the same time restricting its efficient *dissemination*?[1] The solution in this case is arguably to give insurers private property rights over the use of the information they gather, with the expectation that they will use them to secure improvements in risk management which are in the interest of the public. The difficulty with this solution, however, is that each individual insurer may not have sufficient data to generate reliable guidance for risk management activities. When insurers' portfolios are small relative to the diverse nature of the risk, it is possible that their claims experience is inadequate to derive actuarial benefit. A highly concentrated insurance market is one response to this problem, but this would also reduce the competitive pressure to use information productively.

The consequence of this logic is that the role of risk management may need to be separated from the role of insurance, and it may be that the former would require a co-ordinated approach to claims information by, or on behalf of, the insured community. Moreover, the separation of the two objectives would permit a less constrained approach to the type of information to be collected: it would be desirable to collect data on all incidents which potentially could lead to medical accidents, not just those which resulted in a claim.

In the light of these issues, this chapter reviews the background to the development and use of medical claims databases in the UK and the US. It also uses data from existing surveys of claims to illustrate the potential advantages from such databases, and incidentally to compare as far as possible the salient characteristics of medical litigation in the two countries.

RECENT UK EXPERIENCE

Prior to 1 January 1990, the position in the UK was one of very weak incentives to make constructive use of claims data. Clinicians were insured against medical negligence through one of three defence organizations, whereas hospitals, as agents of government bodies, self-insured. The defence organizations did not relate their subscriptions to variations in risk by specialty or otherwise. Consequently there was little pressure from insured clinicians for information on risk management: the incentive to identify high risk areas of medicine was diluted to the extent that any reduced premiums would be spread over all the membership.[2] The defence organizations had databases, but access to these was severely restricted as a result of their commercial concern about potential competition.

The health authorities, as employers of hospital doctors, also had databases on claims. These varied considerably in the way in which the data were collected and used, and were often highly decentralized, at district or even unit level. As a consequence there was little perceived benefit from their use as management information systems.

After 1 January 1990, the Department of Health decided to indemnify all their hospital and community health service employees against liability for medical negligence. General practitioners and hospital clinicians who worked outside the NHS would continue to need cover through the defence organizations (or other insurers), as would all doctors for care given outside their contracts, such as roadside treatment to accident victims. However, to all intents and purposes it is now the health authorities which bear liability for medical negligence. The implications of this development for the use of claims data are not yet clear. On the one hand, the *number* of claims which are the sole responsibility of health authorities has increased significantly, thereby increasing the managerial incentive to minimize risk of litigation. On the other hand, the Department has encouraged district health authorities to adopt a decentralized approach to claims management, with the result that the relevant data may still be collected at a very low level of aggregation.[3] The defence organizations and independent firms of solicitors may well react to the new situation by offering claims management services incorporating the establishment and maintenance of databases, but this prospect has yet to be clarified. A recent Royal College of Physicians Working Party, in recommending the establishment of a national claims database, has called for DHAs to 'coordinate their approaches to this problem, either in conjunction with the defence organizations, or through the Department of Health' (Royal College of Physicians 1990: 22).

RECENT US EXPERIENCE

While the extent of medical litigation in the US is far greater than in the UK, both in terms of frequency and severity, the competitive nature of both health care and liability insurance markets means that the collection of claims-related data is more diffuse.[4] The leading insurer, the St Paul, uses its own data on the pattern of litigation to advise both physician and hospital policy-holders of the advantages of risk management. Moreover, many of the commercial liability insurers as well as the physician-owned mutuals in the US now require formal risk management programmes as a condition of coverage, which itself has provided a stimulus for the growth and development of individual claims databases.

Notwithstanding these developments, there remains an interest in obtaining information at a more aggregative level in connection with medical claims experience. The General Accounting Office (GAO) survey of the litigation experience of six states in 1984 has been widely cited in this respect, and this has been supplemented by data collected by the Florida Governor's Review of the Insurance and Tort Systems (1987) and the Harvard Medical Practice Study (1990) for New York. In addition, a National Practitioner Data Bank has been established under the Health Care Quality Improvement Act of 1986, in which all malpractice settlements and judgments and disciplinary actions against practitioners are recorded. However, the information on this databank is confidential, and is intended for use in professional peer review as well as in the monitoring of mobile practitioners.

THE OXFORD REGIONAL HEALTH AUTHORITY STUDY

During 1987–88 we were able to obtain access to an extensive series of case files when Oxford Regional Health Authority commissioned us to review all the records available in the region of closed claims alleging negligence by hospital or community medical staff to see what could be learnt from the aggregate picture. Since health authorities were, at that time, normally joined in any action for negligence against any doctor whom they employed, this should present a complete picture of claims arising from NHS services in the region. The series excludes private practice, but this is not a high-volume activity and defence society officials state that it has a relatively low incidence of claims. The study also omits general practitioner services provided under contract to the NHS, but these again are said not to generate a significant number of claims.

Oxford Region is reasonably typical of non-metropolitan areas of Britain, although its relative affluence and lack of heavy industry contribute to a better-than-average mortality and morbidity record. In terms of claim rates, it seems to lie close to the national median at 7.8 per 100,000 population.

At the time of the study the Region was unusual in delegating responsibility for managing negligence claims to district level, instead of centralizing them, either through an in-house legal department or through a retainer with a single outside law firm. However, this has now become the Department of Health's preferred model, with the introduction in 1990 of the NHS indemnity scheme under which DHAs assume responsibility for all liability claims made against their medical employees in hospital and community services.[5] Indeed, it has recently been announced that responsibility for claims management is to be decentralized even further, with individual hospitals rather than DHAs bearing liability, and passing the cost of this on to the purchasers of health care via the cost of their contracts.[6]

Each district in the Oxford Region had its own private legal advisers and its own arrangements for claims management. Most collected their claims at the district office, but others kept them at individual units. The best-documented districts had what appeared to be complete record series since the 1974 reorganization. Others were more fragmentary, often scattered across a number of locations as a result of changes in district organization and management policy. Most districts, though, had clearly tightened their practice since about 1980–81 and given more attention to the compilation and maintenance of the materials. We have much greater confidence in the data from that period onwards.

This picture of disarray, of course, sends its own message about the importance with which these files were regarded as a source of information and about potential problems for the operation of NHS indemnity. As we learned from the staff involved, claims were managed on a case-by-case basis. Each was treated as a one-off event, resisted or settled and closed. Only one district produced any kind of statistical summary, although another was in the process of creating a small computerized database which would allow it to do the same.

In fairness to the districts, the benefits from collecting such data were far from clear. The district with the largest number of closed claims had still only experienced 115 over the period 1980–88. Most were in a range of 30–60 claims closed in that time. Statistical analysis of such small numbers would have been unlikely to yield any worthwhile information. When aggregated to regional level, however, we were able to identify 470 cases, which became the basis of our study. Even this, in fact, is too small a number for any degree of specificity. As implied above, if tort claims are to be used in medical risk management, and to contribute effectively to the process of quality assurance in the NHS, arrangements will have to be made to collect reports on a much larger scale.

A COMPARATIVE ANALYSIS OF CLAIMS EXPERIENCE

The extraction of data from the original records in Oxford employed a modified version of a protocol developed by the Risk Management Foundation of the Harvard Hospitals, which also forms the basis of the extraction scheme used in the study by the US General Accounting Office (1987) of a national sample of 25 insurers' records of 2,781 medical negligence claims closed in 1984.[7] While the data are not absolutely comparable, because of the exclusions from the Oxford series and detailed differences in the coding, it is possible to identify a number of gross differences which may form the basis of further investigations.[8] In particular, the comparison allows us to examine whether patients are claiming for the same sorts of injuries and professional failures in each country, but at a higher rate in the USA, or whether the difference in rates is attributable to a different pattern of claims.

Who claims?

The Oxford files contained very little information about claimants, although it is possible that more could have been obtained if we had been permitted to link them to clinical records. We were only able to analyse the claim records by sex and age. It seems that the General Accounting Office study ran into similar problems and only published a breakdown by sex. There is virtually no difference in the sex ratio of the claimant population in the two series with about 57 per cent of women and 43 per cent of men in each. The excess in claims from women in England does not seem to be wholly explained by their greater use of health services: in 1985 they accounted for 53.3 per cent of all spells in NHS hospitals (Department of Health 1988, Table 4.1) but the difference is not large and may simply be a matter of regional variation. American claimants were rather more likely to end up with some payment but the prospects of success did not vary significantly with the sex of the plaintiff.

The limitations of the information meant we were only able to make a crude age breakdown of the Oxford series into children (16.8 per cent), adults of working age (70.4 per cent) and the retired (12.7). None of these was related to the prospects of success. When compared with hospital activity data for 1985, however, it does seem that elderly people are not represented among claimants in proportion to their representation in the patient population: 12.7 per cent of claimants and 32.4 per cent of spells in hospital (Lord Chancellor's Department 1988, Table 4.1). Claims from children are more or less in proportion to their spells in hospital (15.7 per cent), although one might have expected a slightly higher rate as a result of their heavier usage of community health services. Most of the excess, then, seems to come from adults of working age, who are likely, as a group, to experience the greatest economic losses from any medical misadventure.

Who is claimed against?

It is well known that the prospects of being sued vary significantly by specialty. Table 1.1 sets out for each country the claims experience of the five most frequently sued specialties. In each case the figures relate to hospital doctors only, and exclude multiple defendant cases.

Table 1.1 Claims and payments by specialty

Specialty	Total claims (% of total)		Claims paid (%)	
	UK	US	UK	US
Anaesthesiology	6.8	4.9	51.6	53.8
General surgery	10.3	13.9	34.0	34.1
Obstetrics and gynaecology	22.0	14.3	25.0	55.7
Orthopaedic surgery	15.6	9.7	32.4	46.8
Accident and emergency	10.8	5.4	34.7	29.4
Other	34.5	51.8	33.8	45.5
Total	100.0	100.0	33.0	42.3

It can be seen that there is more dispersal of claims in the US, where these five specialties only acccount for half of all claims, while they make up almost two-thirds of the cases in the Oxford series. The latter seems to reveal relatively high proportions in obstetrics and gynaecology, orthopaedics and accident work, although it is not clear that this is entirely comparable with the US category of emergency medicine. Turning to the proportion of cases which are paid, we can see that the overall likelihood of success is significantly higher in the US: at 42.3 per cent compared to 33 per cent in the UK. Anaesthetic cases have a better than average chance of success in both countries, but the picture is different for other specialties. In the US, emergency and general surgery claims are less likely to succeed than average, while in the Oxford Region claimants have about an average chance of success. There is, however, a marked difference in the prospects of obstetric/gynaecology and orthopaedic claims, both of which have a better than average chance of success in the US and are much lower than average and average respectively in Oxford.

What do people claim for?

It is when we come to examine the events which provoke claims that the limitations of even the largest database become apparent. One of the most striking features of both the Oxford Region and the GAO series is the sheer diversity of the incidents which they cover. The ten most common allegations in each country only account for something like half the cases in the UK and two-thirds in the US, and even this result is achieved by constructing some loose categories like 'Improper performance of surgery' which could embrace a wide variety of occurrences.

There are two obvious differences between the experiences of Oxford and the USA. One is the importance of claims relating to problems of diagnosis in the American data – 28 per cent of all claims compared with 12 per cent in Oxford. The other is the considerable difference in the proportion of claims relating to treatment – 13.9 per cent in the USA and 7.7 per cent in Oxford. It is possible that these results simply reflect different drafting conventions in the two countries' legal professions. Alternatively, they may indicate that English patients are willing to accept a more measured approach to diagnosis and that English hospital organization makes it possible to exercise greater supervision of the treatment prescribed by physicians, although not, evidently, by surgeons (where the proportion of claims was remarkably similar – 21.8 per cent in the UK and 22.2 per cent in the US).

From the point of view of risk management, however, the dispersal of events blurs any signal that might be generated by claim frequency alone.

Table 1.2 Claims and payments by principal allegations: UK

Principal allegations	Total claims (% of total)	Claims paid (%)
1 Surgery: improper performance	17.4	30.4
2 Failure to diagnose	10.5	33.3
3 Treatment: other error	4.2	20.0
4 Obstetrics: wrongful life	4.0	11.1
5 Treatment: improper performance	3.5	50.0
6 Surgery: foreign body left	2.9	53.8
7 Obstetrics: improper management	2.2	10.0
8 Anaesthetics: improper equipment	2.2	50.0
9 Delayed diagnosis	1.5	14.3
10 Surgery: unnecessary	1.5	42.9
Other	50.1	
Total	100.0	33.0

Table 1.3 Claims and payments by principal allegations: US

Principal allegations	Total claims (% of total)	Claims paid (%)
1 Surgery: improper performance	17.4	39.6
2 Failure to diagnose	12.4	50.5
3 Misdiagnosis	10.2	30.7
4 Treatment: improper performance	8.2	40.7
5 Delayed diagnosis	5.4	44.1
6 Treatment: improper choice	3.5	44.0
7 Surgery: unnecessary	2.4	27.5
8 Surgery: other error	2.4	46.6
9 Treatment: failure to render	2.2	15.0
10 Wrong dosage order	1.8	23.7
Other	34.1	
Total	100.0	43.2

There are some differences in the success rates of claims which might be used as a weighting factor. However, there is no clear pattern in the likelihood of success. In Oxford those allegations which had a low chance of success were those involving obstetrics and diagnostic delay; a high chance of success was found in anaesthetics, improper performance of treatment, and where foreign bodies were alleged to have been left by surgeons. In the US, success was relatively less likely for failure to render treatment or wrong dosage orders; and relatively more likely for failed diagnosis.

An alternative approach to the problem of priorities in risk management, which looks more closely at the relationship between the tort system and the compensation needs of patients, is to consider the severity of the injuries.

The main feature of Table 1.4 is the remarkable similarity between the severity profiles of claimants in the two countries, in contrast to the frequently heard assertion that Americans are inclined to pursue frivolous or trivial cases because of the contingency fee system. Indeed, Table 1.4 shows that, if anything, American claimants are more seriously injured on average, with the proportion of 'insignificant' or 'emotional' injuries being 13.7 per cent in the US, compared with 21.8 per cent in Oxford. As we have observed elsewhere (Fenn and Dingwall 1990), the assertion of excessive US litigiousness has never been consistent with the fact that lawyers are unlikely to risk their own money on cases which are too uncertain or low in value to promise them a reasonable return on their investment. The results

Table 1.4 Claims and payments by severity

Severity of injury	Total claims (% of total)		Claims paid (%)	
	UK	US	UK	US
Emotional	7.8	5.4	23.5	24.6
Insignificant	14.0	8.3	41.0	52.7
Temporary minor	26.0	29.7	32.7	37.0
Temporary major	12.2	11.1	41.5	35.3
Permanent partial minor	16.1	16.0	44.3	52.2
Permanent partial major	6.2	5.4	29.6	50.4
Permanent total major	3.4	3.6	13.3	68.2
Permanent total grave	1.6	2.9	28.6	80.7
Death	12.2	17.3	22.6	39.0
Other	0.5	0.4	50.0	3.8
Total	100.0	100.0	34.0	43.2

here provide further evidence for questioning the conventional wisdom. There may well be more litigation in the US, but the litigants themselves appear to have cases which are in no way weaker, or more 'trivial', than in the UK.

There is, however, an evident difference in the pattern of claimant success between the two countries in relation to the severity of the claimant's injury. In the UK, while the success rate of claimants varies among severity categories, there appears to be no systematic tendency for the more severe injuries to be more successful. By contrast, in the US, there is a fairly clear gradation, with 'emotional' injuries succeeding in only 24.6 per cent of claims, whereas 'permanent total grave' injuries succeed in over 80 per cent of cases. It is possible that this difference between the two countries reflects the impact of jury trials in the US, and a consequent belief in that country that it will be very difficult to defend an action where the events alleged have led to the serious injury or permanent disability of a patient which is likely to arouse the lay person's sympathy whatever the technical merits of the case.

Damages and costs

The GAO study was able to compile more detailed analyses of costs and damages than was possible from the Oxford Region data. However, a number of broad comparisons can still be made. Table 1.5 presents the evidence on damages and costs.

Table 1.5 Damages and costs by category

	Mean payments UK 1986 (£)	*Mean payments US 1984 ($)*
Total damages	7,293	83,581
Medical expenses		17,773
Lost wages		6,440
Other economic loss		6,263
Non-economic loss		50,375
Pre-judgment interest		145
Total plaintiff costs	1,418	29,385
Total defendant costs[9]	713	7,019

The sums in Table 1.5 are given in each country's own currency for the years stated. When converted at an exchange rate typical for the mid-1980s (£1 = $1.6), the differences in total damages and costs are considerable. Average total damages in the US of $84,000 (£53,000) compare with £7,300 ($11,700) in Oxford – some 14 per cent of the American level. It is, however, important to recognize that the damage awards are not strictly comparable. Some allowance needs to be made for contingency fees, relative earnings levels and living costs in the two countries, as well as the differential costs of private health care. If such calculations were possible, it seems likely that the residual difference would be largely attributable to different attitudes towards the compensation of non-economic losses. As Table 1.5 clearly shows, these are typically very substantial in the US, comprising some 60 per cent of the total award. Again, one suspects the influence of a jury system, although it is surely a fine argument as to whether a panel of lay persons or a judge is better qualified to value pain and suffering, as opposed to the estimation of lost wages or housing costs. The absence of punitive damages in the American figures underline their irrelevance in medical cases, which has also been reported by Daniels and Martin (1990).

The other striking feature is the contrast in plaintiffs' legal costs: in the USA these amounted to 35 per cent of the total recovered while in Oxford the mean was just under 20 per cent. Defendants' costs do not show the same pattern, though, amounting to 13 per cent of recoveries in the USA and 14 per cent in the UK.[10] This kind of imbalance is not untypical of personal injury litigation, since defendants are likely to enjoy some economies of scale and effort from their position as repeat players. What may be more interesting is to consider who is spending the 'right' amount on the plaintiff's side. Is the US figure inflated by contingency fees or does the UK figure actually suggest an underinvestment in the case which may lead to skimped preparation and presentation? It is also notable that these percentages do not support some of the wilder assertions about the costs of tort claims for medical injuries. While some cases may be very costly to pursue, the mean in Oxford is considerably lower than that reported by the Inbucon study of personal injury cases for the Civil Justice Review which reported that the average plaintiff's costs were about 35 per cent of the damages in High Court actions (Lord Chancellor's Department 1988, para 2.3). The same study found defendants' costs averaging 24 to 36 per cent, depending upon where the case was heard.

Table 1.6 shows the variation in costs and damages for the five most claim-prone specialties in the US and England. One striking difference shown by Table 1.6 is the relatively high costs and damages of obstetrics and gynaecology cases in the US compared to those in England. It is likely, however, that the low levels of damages in Oxford is because of the fortuitous absence, during the period of our study, of any large payout in a 'brain-damaged baby' case; such cases have become more frequent in recent years. But this, in itself, indicates their comparative rarity in the past in the experience of any individual district. Large awards in England may be lost in the noise of a high rate of low-value settlements and abandoned claims which incur few legal expenses.

Table 1.6 Damages and costs by specialty

Specialty	Mean damages		Mean defendant's costs	
	UK (£)	US ($)	UK (£)	US ($)
Anaesthesiology	2,761	50,274	1,045	2,986
General surgery	4,217	62,053	1,826	7,555
Obstetrics and gynaecology	3,926	186,216	492	14,455
Orthopaedic surgery	10,080	114,769	676	9,539
Accident and emergency	12,700	26,393	368	7,255
Total	7,292	83,581	713	7,019

Tables 1.7 and 1.8 show the levels of damages and defendant's costs for each of the ten most frequent allegations in the two countries. In both countries, the two most frequent allegations – improper per- formance of surgery and failure to diagnose – were also among the most costly to the defendants in terms of damages awarded. Similarly, treatment error and the more minor surgical errors were relatively low cost allegations in both countries. The main exception to this pattern is with the allegation of improper choice of treatment in the US, which shows the highest mean damage award of all. Interestingly, in neither country did the level of defendant's costs bear a close relationship to the level of damages awarded, which seems to suggest that the complexity and duration of cases are determined by factors other than the nature of the alleged medical error.

CONCLUSION

This chapter began by noting the difficulties in using information on medical negligence claims for risk management purposes when that information is collected in a decentralized manner. It was argued that, in

Table 1.7 Damages and costs by principal allegations: UK

Principal allegations	Mean damages (£)	Mean defendant's costs † (£)
1 Surgery: improper performance	10,205	529
2 Failure to diagnose	13,133	731
3 Treatment: other error	1,720	526
4 Obstetrics: wrongful life	8,165	259
5 Treatment: improper performance	1,535	883
6 Surgery: foreign body left	911	224
7 Obstetrics: improper management	*	565
8 Anaesthetics: improper equipment	*	*
9 Delayed diagnosis	*	858
10 Surgery: unnecessary	*	690
Total	7,293	713

* Insufficient paid claims to yield reliable estimates.
† Defence costs for health authority only.

Table 1.8 Damages and costs by principal allegations: US

Principal allegations	Mean damages ($)	Mean defendant's costs ($)
1 Surgery: improper performance	101,104	6,536
2 Failure to diagnose	98,676	8,567
3 Treatment: improper performance	32,832	3,245
4 Misdiagnosis	63,977	7,115
5 Delayed diagnosis	52,398	7,577
6 Treatment: improper choice	160,28	5,294
7 Treatment: failure to render	29,270	4,401
8 Surgery: other error	6,117	1,664
9 Surgery: unnecessary	10,427	17,518
10 Wrong dosage order	15,066	1,223
Total	83,581	7,019

those circumstances, the tort system is characterized by random, weak and diffuse signals which give little or no worthwhile guidance to individuals or institutions about quality investment. It is only when data are collected at the most aggregate levels that the signals become any clearer, although difficulties remain in relation to the identification of events considered to be 'failures' in medical practice.

The chapter then undertook a cross-national comparison based on results from two surveys of claims: one over a large number of insurers' claims experience in the US for a particular year; the other over a large number of years for a particular health authority's claims in the UK. It would be fair to conclude that neither survey is sufficiently large to permit the rigorous testing of hypotheses relating to the medical processes and clinical activity most likely to lead to patient injury, thus perhaps emphasizing our initial point. However, the evidence presented here does identify some clear differences in the costs associated with each system, as represented by legal expenses and the payment of damages. It also points up some additional areas which might repay further investigation, such as the apparent tendency of US physicians to encounter a high rate of claims relating to diagnosis rather than treatment, although it is not clear whether this represents a real difference or whether it is because of different conventions in the drafting of claims by US and UK lawyers.

Despite these notes of caution, some of the results presented here point in directions that might lead to a more constructive approach to outcome-based quality control in the health sector. Bringing together information on the frequency of claims, their likelihood of success and their relative severity – as measured by both the nature of the injury and its settlement value – can provide guidance as to those specialties and areas of potential clinical error which should be targeted for greatest effectiveness. It is possible that only the close monitoring of the processes of health care, alongside its outcomes, will provide sufficient information for this purpose. We would argue that this is an area in which it could be uncontroversially said that the more information, the better the care.

NOTES

1 See Hirshleifer (1971) for a discussion of this issue in the broader context.
2 Interestingly, towards the end of this period, there were signs that the increasing average subscription levels, combined with the threat of competitive entry to the insurance market, were beginning to change attitudes in this respect.
3 Indeed, this has been reinforced following the recent health service reforms by the decision of the NHS Management Executive to introduce principles of accounting at unit level (i.e. individual hospitals), which will result in the costs of medical negligence claims being borne by the units concerned (both NHS

trusts and directly managed units), and subsequently reflected in their financial reporting and pricing decisions.

4 The degree of competition between liability insurers should not be exaggerated, however. Most insurance is provided on a programme basis sponsored by local or state medical societies. Individual policies represent a relatively minor segment of the market, and companies who offer such policies use the rating services of the Insurance Services Office (ISO). See Danzon (1985) for an account of the malpractice insurance market.

5 Prior to this scheme, doctors were required, as a condition of employment in NHS hospital or community medical services, to carry private liability insurance obtained from one of the medical defence organizations. These have the legal status of friendly societies but for present purposes can be thought of as a type of physician-owned mutual insurer. Negligence claims arising from NHS work would normally join the individual doctor and the employing authority, who would then negotiate with the defence organization about the potential division of liability and the responsibility for leading the defence or settlement of the case. Under NHS indemnity, the health service assumes full vicarious liability for the actions of its medical staff, as it always has done for other employees. General practitioners and doctors in private practice continue, of course, to make independent arrangements for liability insurance through their membership of the defence organizations (Fenn and Dingwall 1990).

6 See note 3 above.

7 This sample was drawn from an estimated total of 73,472 claims closed by 102 insurance companies (US GAO 1987, p. 18).

8 Figures for the US in this chapter are based on direct analysis of the GAO database, kindly made available to us by Professor Russell Localio of the Harvard School of Public Health. The data are weighted to reflect the sampling procedures applied to the 25 participating insurance companies. Minor differences between the results reported here and those published in the GAO Report (GAO 1987) probably reflect different assumptions relating to the construction of subsets of defendants.

9 These figures represent the mean defendant's costs per *claimant* (reflecting the fact that even unpaid claims involve some costs); the mean defendant's costs per *paid claim* were £1,323 in the UK and $10,433 in the US.

10 It should be borne in mind, however, that the UK figures represent health authority costs only. In some cases in our sample there will have been supplementary legal expenses incurred by the clinician's legal representatives (i.e. the medical defence societies).

2 Medical discipline in cross-cultural perspective
The United States, Britain and Sweden

Marilynn M. Rosenthal

The increasing international interest in medical malpractice issues has focused long overdue attention on the disciplinary mechanisms that exist for receiving complaints against medical practitioners and administering discipline, where deemed appropriate. It is particularly informative to look at these mechanisms in cross-cultural perspective, providing an opportunity for greater objectivity in assessing organizational features, decision-making processes, outcomes and general effectiveness in accomplishing goals.

In Britain, the General Medical Council, a statutory professional organi-zation, has responsibility for maintaining standards of medical education, registering doctors to practise medicine, and receiving and processing complaints against the medical profession. The Council's right to discipline doctors flows from its licensing powers. There are two other mechanisms of discipline: Family Practitioner Committees (now Family Health Services Authorities) can fine general practitioners for breaches of their contracts with the National Health Service, and the Regional Medical Officer can suspend and dismiss a hospital doctor. The present discussion will focus on the functions of the General Medical Council, since it is the only body which has the right to revoke registration.

In Sweden, the licensing and discipline functions are conducted by two distinct government bodies. The National Board of Health and Welfare carries out the licensing process while a free-standing administrative agency, the Medical Responsibility Board, processes complaints and dis-penses sanctions where appropriate. It does this for all health professions, not just doctors.

In the United States, both licensing and disciplinary activities are carried out on the state level by the same public agency, usually a state Board of Medicine with separate licensing and discipline offices.

Having noted the differences between the three countries, professional control in Britain and public control in Sweden and the United States, it will be informative to compare and contrast the organization of these activities, the disciplinary issues addressed, decision-making and the role played as agents of regulation and quality assurance in medical care.

THE AMERICAN APPROACH

The processing of complaints against doctors and the right to discipline is a state function in the United States carried out by fifty different state medical licensing and disciplinary boards. Their purpose is to try to ensure competency among medical professionals. While they are the single official public agency empowered to receive complaints against physicians and impose sanctions, they have been singularly ineffective and increasingly criticized. Although they are governmental units, they have been dominated by members of the medical profession and have had little public representation. Recent public pressure has led to some accelerated activity.

The individual state legislatures grant the disciplinary powers of all licensing boards and committees under police powers guaranteed to the states in the Tenth Amendment to the US Constitution. Portions of all state Medical Practice Acts list the offences for which a board can punish a physician; most such offences fall under the heading of 'unprofessional conduct'.

The only comprehensive study of US state medical boards was published in 1979 (Grad and Marti 1979). It surveyed all the boards and provided particularly detailed information on nine selected states although data-gathering for all parts of the study was constrained because little information was systematically kept. The types of actions state boards could take included reprimand, censure, fines, probation, limitation of practice, imposition of educational or retraining requirements, uncompensated public service, suspension or revocation of licence to practise. The nine-state study revealed that reprimand, probation, suspension and revocation of licence were the types of sanction most often imposed. Most complaints came from the general public, although some states required by statute that medical societies, hospitals, insurance companies, clerks of courts, malpractice arbitration panels or fellow physicians report various behaviours or violations.

In the nine selected states, the largest proportion of cases taken on were related to drug and alcohol abuse and unlawful prescribing. In the state of New York, half the cases were concerned with 'professional misconduct'. The state boards generally met once a month in their offices with varying degrees of public access. The meetings resembled courts of law, following legal rules of evidence, due process, right to counsel for all parties, right to cross-examination, subpoena power, and right to appeal and judicial review.

According to Robert Derbyshire (1983), former director of the Federation of State Medical Boards, the state Medical Practice Acts which shape the work of the disciplinary boards are inadequate for several reasons. First, there is no single, consistent definition of the types of offence calling for disciplinary action. Second, states cannot agree on the causes or reasons for the imposition of sanctions against physicians. And finally, a result of the lack of uniformity of sanctions (a major defect in the laws of all except fifteen states) is 'state hopping' of delinquent physicians who hold multiple licences. There is no clause in the laws providing for suspension or revocation of a licence if another state board has taken action based upon an act similar to one specified in the law of the original state. This defect has been partially addressed through the creation in 1989 of a new federal agency, the National Practitioner Data Bank. All state licensing and discipline boards (and other organizations) must now report licence suspensions and revocations. Neither the boards nor health care providers are, however, obliged to consult the clearing house database before granting licensure, hospital privileges or HMO membership to a doctor moving into a state.

Because of the perceived inadequacy of the Medical Practice Acts, as well as the fact that the majority of disciplinary board members are physicians, Derbyshire questions the effectiveness of the boards in protecting the public against unscrupulous, unethical and incompetent physicians. He estimates that, of some 450,000 licensed physicians in the United States in 1983, approximately 5 per cent or 22,500 were incompetent or unscrupulous. There were many cases of alcoholism, both detected and undetected, and drug addiction. A large number of physicians also lapsed into senility or obsolescence each year.

Case study: State of Michigan Board of Medicine

For further illustration, several recent studies of licensing in the State of Michigan can be reviewed. Table 2.1 provides an overview of the State of Michigan Board of Medicine. The Michigan Department of Licensing and Regulation is supposed to protect Michigan citizens against bad health practitioners. The department includes thirteen boards that license the state's 170,000 nurses, medical doctors, osteopathic physicians, dentists and other health care professionals. After the Michigan State Board of Medicine (which is made up of ten doctors, a physician's assistant and three persons not in a health care profession) licenses doctors, it is supposed to ensure that they remain at least minimally competent. In practice, however, the board does not monitor all Michigan's doctors. Instead, 'it weighs evidence against those who come to the attention of the Department of Licensing and Regulation because of citizen complaints or

Table 2.1 USA: State of Michigan Board of Medicine (with disciplinary functions)

History	Series of state statutes, most recent enacted in 1978
Composition	10 MDs 1 physician's assistant 3 lay members (who must not be health care professionals)
Self-description	Quasi-legal (administrative law)
Types of issue addressed	1 Unprofessional conduct 2 Failure to use responsible care and discrimination in prescribing of drugs 3 Failure to conform to minimum standards of acceptable and prevailing medical practice
Who disciplined	Doctors
Types of actions possible	1 Reprimand 2 Probation 3 Suspension 4 Revocation 5 Limit practice 6 Require rehabilitation
Sources of complaints	1 Public 2 Medical Society reports 3 Hospitals 4 Insurance companies 5 Clerks of courts
How often meet	Monthly
Where meet	Board of Medicine Office located in state capital, Lansing
Type of meeting	Resembles court of law 1 Notice required 2 Board may administer oaths, subpoena evidence and witnesses 3 Defendant can subpoena witnesses and evidence 4 Hearing conducted by panel composed of 2 members of board and a hearing officer 5 Written decision 6 Appeal rights 7 Judicial review

Source: Rosenthal and Fredericks 1985.

because they have been disciplined by a hospital, sued, or investigated by drug agents' (Katz 1984). About 10 per cent of the complaints received are investigated.

Furthermore, once cases are brought to the board, they take approximately two and a half years to go through the state disciplinary system. One reason the process takes so long is because the department has, until recently, been seriously underfunded. Also, critics of the regulatory system argue that it seems designed more to protect the health care professional's licence than to protect the public's health. Meanwhile, during this long period of time, potentially incompetent physicians continue to practise.

The formal charges against these doctors included (in order of frequency of complaint) irresponsible or illegal drug prescribing, abusing alcohol or drugs, incompetence, fraud, sex with patients and mental illness. Where licences were revoked, four doctors have subsequently been returned, seven have moved their work to another state and seven are no longer practising medicine. Of the ten who were summarily suspended, five have had their licences returned. Of the twelve whose licences were suspended, five have got them back, one is working in another state, four are over 65, and two are not practising any more (Katz 1984).

Often a bad doctor practises for years before the problem even comes to the state's attention. Between 1984 and 1988 the State Board of Medicine took away only between four and nine of the approximately 25,000–28,000 Michigan licences held by doctors (State of Michigan 1990). In short, incompetence is hard to prove because of tradition, the law, the uncertain nature of medicine and the reluctance of doctors to condemn their colleagues.

Activity of all American Boards

As Table 2.2 indicates the activities of all the state disciplinary boards have been highly limited. They punished relatively few offenders and Michigan ranks in the lower half of activity. It was not until 1981 that all states began reporting disciplinary actions to the Federation of State Medical Boards. These figures are far below the 5 per cent estimate of incompetent, unscrupulous physicians quoted earlier by Derbyshire and reflect the disparity in disciplinary actions taken in the different states of the United States.

The Federation also began publishing material on the problems leading to licence revocation. The first compilation listed reasons from the years 1962 to 1973 (Rosenthal 1987/1988). The list is revealing since the majority of reasons do not relate directly to medical negligence. The overwhelming majority of licence revocations concerned professional

Table 2.2 Serious disciplinary actions against MDs by state in the USA: 1982, 1987, 1988

1988	Rank 1987	1982	State	Actual number of doctors disciplined 1988	1987	Serious actions taken per 1,000 MDs 1982	1988	Numbers of doctors 1988
1	8	9	Georgia	90	58	3.3	8.6	10,524
2	7	6	Iowa	37	26	5.5	8.4	4,384
3	11	15	Missouri	79	49	3.0	7.9	9,996
4	10	16	Oklahoma	38	25	3.0	7.6	4,994
5	9	25	Nevada	12	9	2.3	7.2	1,676
6	4	4	Mississippi	24	20	6.0	7.0	3,416
7	18	30	Colorado	42	26	1.8	6.0	7,028
8	1	19	West Virginia	19	29	2.9	5.6	3,381
9	5	32	Hawaii	13	15	1.6	5.2	2,506
10	6	5	South Dakota	5	6	5.9	5.0	1,004
11	25	34	Illinois	126	67	1.2	4.9	25,537
12	24	21	Minnesota	43	28	2.6	4.5	9,535
13	3	37	Kentucky	27	41	1.1	4.4	6,188
14	14	1	Florida	116	129	7.4	4.2	27,851
15	2	23	Alaska	3	5	2.4	4.1	724
16	23	12	New Jersey	74	59	3.1	3.9	18,883
17	21	24	Indiana	34	30	2.3	3.9	8,731
18	19	51	North Dakota	4	4	0.0	3.5	1,136
19	39	10	New Mexico	9	4	3.3	3.3	2,735
20	21	8	South Carolina	18	19	4.4	3.3	5,522
21	16	17	Utah	10	13	3.0	3.2	3,128
22	35	40	Ohio	68	38	0.9	3.1	21,744
23	27	28	Virginia	36	29	1.9	2.9	12,311
24	51	13	Kansas	12	2	3.1	2.7	4,460
25	26	14	Louisiana	21	22	3.1	2.5	8,453
26	48	48	Arkansas	9	3	0.0	2.5	3,664
27	20	43	Massachusetts	47	67	0.7	2.4	19,766
28	44	31	Alabama	15	8	1.8	2.4	6,323
29	33	27	Michigan	40	34	1.9	2.3	17,549
30	17	29	Oregon	13	23	1.9	2.2	5,877
31	32	42	North Carolina	26	22	0.8	2.2	11,783
32	43	22	Maine	5	3	2.6	2.2	2,306
33	47	33	Tennessee	20	8	1.4	2.2	9,285
34	27	50	DC	8	9	0.0	2.1	3,819
35	15	36	New York	98	259	1.1	1.7	57,779
36	36	26	Maryland	25	26	2.0	1.7	15,000
37	50	47	Connecticut	15	7	0.3	1.5	9,833
38	46	46	Pennsylvania	43	27	0.5	1.5	28,476
39	30	11	Idaho	2	3	3.3	1.5	1,341

Table 2.2 Continued

1988	Rank 1987	1982	State	Actual number of doctors disciplined 1988	1987	Serious actions taken per 1,000 MDs 1982	1988	Numbers of doctors 1988
40	40	3	Nebraska	4	5	6.8	1.5	2,762
41	41	7	Wyoming	1	1	4.5	1.4	706
42	34	44	New Hampshire	3	4	0.6	1.4	2,149
43	31	41	Vermont	2	3	0.9	1.4	1,469
44	42	20	California	93	94	2.8	1.3	71,349
45	38	39	Texas	35	43	0.9	1.2	29,207
46	29	35	Washington	11	23	1.2	1.1	10,079
47	12	18	Wisconsin	8	45	2.9	0.9	9,234
48	13	49	Delaware	1	6	0.0	0.8	1,290
49	45	2	Arizona	4	9	7.0	0.6	7,303
50	37	45	Rhode Island	1	4	0.6	0.4	2,489
51	49	38	Montana	0	0	1.0	0.0	1,323
								538,008

Sources: 1982 data: Federation of State Medical Boards. Data represent the number of reported actions and are only approximations because reporting may be incomplete in some states. Reported in 'The ethics of professional regulations', Richard J. Feinstein, MD, *New England Journal of Medicine*, 313, 12 (21 March 1985): 801–4.
1987 and 1988 data: Public Citizen Health Research Group, July 1990, Table 2. Adapted from *Federation Bulletin*, Federation of State Medical Boards, 'Official 1988 federation summary of reported disciplinary actions'.

issues such as non-payment of fees, state issues like failure to obtain citizenship papers and 'unprofessional conduct'. Four per cent were related to narcotics violations. During this time, the US state medical boards were simply not reviewing complaints concerning medical negligence, nor was this a period of particular use of the American courts in medical malpractice cases.

A recent, but more limited, study conducted by the Public Citizen Health Research Group (1990a) looks at the reasons for all disciplinary actions, not just licence revocation. The five leading causes are:

1 overprescribing or misprescribing drugs (20.3 per cent)
2 non-compliance with board order or professional rule (16.4 per cent)
3 criminal conviction (10 per cent)
4 drug or alcohol abuse (9.2 per cent)
5 substandard care or negligence (8.9 per cent).

State of Michigan (1990) figures for the period 1984–85 are rather different:

1 substandard care or negligence (33 per cent)
2 criminal behaviour including convictions (20 per cent)
3 overprescribing or misprescribing (15 per cent)
4 professional misconduct (14 per cent)
5 impairment (6 per cent).

These figures suggest that, since the earlier Federation study, the state boards are taking on more clinical competence cases but are still heavily focused on drug, criminal and non-professional issues.

The disciplinary bodies are not entirely to blame for the relatively large number of incompetent physicians still holding licences. They encounter serious legal and professional obstacles to their work. Doctors remain reluctant to report incompetent colleagues. The boards have to be careful of their own legal liability which can vary from state to state. Some states, like Michigan, have recently passed laws protecting members of the board from legal liability. Legal manoeuvres can prolong hearings for extended periods of time, letting bad doctors continue to practise. Boards are often unable to gain access to patients' records and do not have automatic transfer of information about in-hospital discipline. Hospitals often let bad doctors resign voluntarily and do not automatically pass on information for fear of libel suits.

Recent changes

Recent developments in the United States, and in the State of Michigan, promise to improve the work of the disciplinary boards. More rigorous reporting of malpractice cases has now been mandated. Nationally, the Health Care Quality Improvement Act created the National Practitioner Data Bank in April 1990. The Data Bank is now functioning and will be a centralized, computerized repository of information about disciplinary actions and malpractice payments from all over the country. Reporting is mandatory; seeking information is voluntary. It is hoped that this will prevent doctors who have lost their licence in one state from starting up practice in another.

Nine states, including Michigan, have passed laws or instituted regulations requiring triplicate forms for doctors with permits to prescribe controlled substances. One copy automatically goes to an enforcement agency. The US Drug Enforcement Agency says that there has been a 50 per cent decrease in the number of scripts written for controlled drugs in these states (Public Citizen Health Research Group 1990b).

As Table 2.2 indicates, sanctions imposed by the state disciplinary boards themselves have increased although a recent report from the Office of the Inspector General of the federal Department of Health and Human Services (Kusserow 1990) states that 'state medical boards discipline far fewer physicians than they should'. The chronic problems – lack of resources, limitations on investigative authority, poor information-sharing, lack of standards about medical competence – still seriously hamper their activities. The work of the American state disciplinary boards is slowly improving, but much more needs to be done to make them effective instruments of appropriate discipline.

THE BRITISH APPROACH

In Great Britain the body with major responsibility for hearing complaints against doctors is the General Medical Council (GMC) which also represents the more general interests of the medical profession. A venerable and well-respected organization, it maintains the Register of doctors, inclusion in which permits a doctor to practise medicine. Granted official status in the first parliamentary Medical Act of 1858, the GMC has broad responsibilities for medical education, for the processes of registration and for professional conduct and discipline. Its disciplinary work today is carried out by three committees: the Preliminary Proceedings Committee, the Health Committee and the Professional Conduct Committee (see Table 2.3).

The Professional Conduct Committee

The Professional Conduct Committee (PCC) of the GMC holds hearings three times a year for a period of two weeks each time. It deals with the most serious cases: those involving doctors convicted in the United Kingdom of a criminal offence and those alleged to be guilty of serious professional misconduct. The PCC is empowered to suspend registration for medical practice, impose conditional registration or call for erasure from the Register completely. It is elected annually by the entire membership of the GMC. Twenty members are elected and ten sit in any single case. The twenty include twelve elected members, two lay members and six appointed members.

The hearings resemble a court of law. A formal procedure is carefully followed; legalistic protocols are carefully observed. The standards for proof are the same as in a criminal trial. Lawyers dominate the proceedings. The doctor is 'on trial'; his or her future registration status is at stake. The patient, or patient's family, or whoever is the complainant is a witness in

Table 2.3 British General Medical Council

History	Series of parliamentary Medical Acts, 1858 to present
Composition of disciplinary committees	Physicians and lay members elected by GMC Professional Conduct Committee (PCC) (20 members, including 2 lay) Preliminary Proceedings Committee (PPC) (11 members) Health Committee
How financed	Member registration and annual retention fees
Type of issue addressed	1 Neglect or disregard of personal responsibility to patients for care and treatment 2 Abuse of professional privileges or skills 3 Conduct derogatory to the reputation of the profession
Who disciplined	Doctors
Types of action possible	1 Letter of advice or no action 2 Admonish and conclude case 3 Warning 4 Probation by postponement 5 Conditional registration 6 Suspension from Register 7 Erasure from Register 8 Referral to Health Committee (since 1980) 9 Restricted prescribing rights
Sources of complaints	Individuals Family Practitioner Committees through the Department of Health and Social Security (DHSS) National Health Service (NHS) hospital authorities The courts
How often meet	Three times a year
Where meet	In chambers of General Medical Council (partially public)
Type of meeting	Resembles court of law 1 Accused has lawyer 2 Accused and complainant cross-examined by GMC lawyer and committee 3 Accused can appeal

Note: Family Practitioner Committees now renamed Family Health Services Authorities. Department of Health and Social Security now split into Department of Health and Department of Social Security.

the case against the doctor, not the plaintiff. Other relevant witnesses also appear, although their numbers are kept to a minimum.

The GMC solicitor asks the majority of questions; the doctor's solicitor or counsel may also examine witnesses. What is missing is the opportunity for those bringing complaints to have a legal representative. The GMC solicitor does not represent the complainant's position and it is his responsibility to see that all the facts are properly established so that the PCC can make an informed decision. The Committee is highly constrained by the structure and protocols of the hearing in developing its response to a complaint.

Any conviction of a doctor by a criminal court in Britain gives the PCC jurisdiction, but the committee is particularly concerned 'with convictions for offences which affect a doctor's fitness to practise' (General Medical Council 1983). The working definition of 'serious professional misconduct' is based on the decisions in two court cases, from 1894 and 1930. These establish the term as referring to behaviour 'regarded as disgraceful or dishonourable by his professional brethren of good repute and competency' (Allinson v General Council for Medical Education and Registration [1894] 1 Q.B. 750 per Lopes L.J.) which is to be 'judged according to the rules, written or unwritten, governing the profession' (R v General Medical Council ex p. Kynaston [1930] 1 K.B. 562 per Scrutton L.J. at 569).

All definitions, rules, regulations and procedures are described in a booklet published by the GMC called *Professional Conduct and Discipline: Fitness to Practise.* This 'Blue Book' also offers advice on specific standards of professional conduct and on medical ethics. Four categories of 'forms of Professional Misconduct which may lead to Disciplinary Proceedings' include: 1) neglect or disregard of personal responsibilities to patients for their care and treatment (examples of this border on what would be called malpractice in the United States); 2) abuse of professional privileges or skills; 3) conduct derogatory to the reputation of the profession (e.g. drug and alcohol abuse, dishonesty, indecency and violence); and 4) advertising, canvassing and related professional offences.

What is most striking is that the major disciplinary body hearing complaints against doctors in Great Britain has not addressed complaints involving clinical negligence. Some cases certainly come close. This is an important point and reveals an essential characteristic of how the GMC has approached its disciplinary functions.

Historic overview of the GMC's disciplinary work

The first Medical Act, in 1858, recognized the right of the medical profession to self-regulation. The disciplinary functions of the GMC received relatively low priority in its early years. However, certain disciplinary practices were established at that time which are still influential today. Section 29 of the Medical Act 1858 stated that registered medical practitioners convicted of any felony or misdemeanour could be erased from the Register if the GMC saw fit. This provision established a pattern whereby, to this day, the courts automatically inform the GMC of such convictions (Varlam 1978).

Between 1858 and 1884 the major disciplinary issue was who was a duly qualified practitioner. By the turn of the century the focus changed to qualifications of medical assistants. By 1915 major disciplinary efforts were focused on doctors employing unqualified assistants, canvassing, advertising, guilty of sexual misconduct, issuing false (illness) certificates and performing abortions.

Some time was required for a legal framework to emerge within which the GMC could carry out its disciplinary tasks. This framework was finally established by the case of *Allinson v General Council for Medical Education and Registration* ([1894] 1 Q.B. 750) in which the courts defined 'infamous' medical conduct and held that they would not intervene to review the Council's interpretation unless there was evidence of bad faith.

Such were the disciplinary concerns of the GMC in the first eighty years of its work. Disciplinary concerns changed as the profession evolved, tried to protect its public image, to define acceptable professional behaviour and to protect the public from those whom it considered unqualified practitioners. Many of these original disciplinary concerns still appear in the GMC's work. Some are now being challenged as inappropriate, and new issues are being suggested for the GMC. It is likely that the next medical Act will broaden the remit of the disciplinary activities to include clinical negligence.

The Preliminary Proceedings Committee

Known before 1978 as the Penal Cases Committee, the Preliminary Proceedings Committee (PPC) serves as a gatekeeper to the disciplinary machinery of the GMC. It reviews court convictions that involve doctors, complaints and letters of inquiry that have been culled by the administrative staff and by the GMC chair, who serves as a 'preliminary screener'. The PPC, meeting in private session, decides which court convictions and which complaints of alleged serious professional misconduct should be referred to either the Health Committee or the Professional Conduct Committee.

Where a referral is not deemed appropriate, the Preliminary Proceedings Committee can warn a doctor concerning questionable conduct and advise on a better standard of behaviour. It can also simply offer general advice and ignore, by putting aside, a complaint.

The Health Committee

This committee was created by the Medical Act 1978 and began operating in August 1980. Its function is to assist a doctor who is seriously impaired physically or mentally. Technically, it can compel a doctor to undergo a medical examination and accept medical supervision and treatment although it attempts to do this through persuasion. If the doctor accepts voluntarily, there is no requirement to appear before the committee or to stop practising. Lack of co-operation could necessitate more formal action and sanctions on practice.

The Health Committee is viewed as a significant improvement over previous arrangements which thrust sick doctors through the formal disciplinary committee structure. A national counselling service to assist sick doctors has recently been established. This, it is hoped, will diminish the need for referral to the GMC.

GMC Professional Conduct Committee decision-making

An analysis of GMC documents (Rosenthal 1987/1988) provides enough information to discern the following patterns:

1 The number of complaints to the GMC has slowly risen in the last two decades but the number taken on as serious cases for hearings has remained relatively constant, even going down in 1988 and 1989.
2 Very few doctors receive the severest sanctions and their numbers are actually shrinking as a proportion of all doctors. The number of erasures from the Register, however, actually doubled in 1988 and 1989.
3 Most cases continue to focus on professional issues rather than clinical skills.
4 The majority of cases concern general practitioners, a significant proportion of them being 'overseas doctors'.

Discussion

The number of doctors in the system has increased, as has the volume of complaints, not only to the GMC but also to the various other organizations that take complaints. This rise is a reflection of a better educated and more assertive public and more media discussion of these issues. The reports of the medical defence organizations reveal a striking increase in court settlements. Yet the number of cases taken on by the GMC has remained relatively static.

The rate at which cases are taken up is closely related to the resources available for their processing: staff, time, money, protocols. The GMC's review must always be constrained by resource limitations. Therefore, its functions are symbolic, signalling to both the profession and the public that it is the guardian of appropriate professional behaviour. There are too many uncertainties in the necessary chain of events for it to be otherwise. These uncertainties include: What is unacceptable behaviour? Will patients understand proper procedures? Will the case be taken up?

As a response to mounting external pressures, the GMC is taking on more cases of 'neglect or disregard of personal responsibility to patients for care and treatment'. This is the closest the GMC comes to what is called malpractice in the USA. Media exposure, parliamentary interest, increased public discussion and the recommendations of its own internal committee have led the GMC to take on more such cases as well as cases involving repeated mistakes (see Table 2.5, p.47). However, the GMC is still clinging to the focus on 'serious professional misconduct', its traditional concern.

For reasons that are not clear (and which require further research), the number of cases resulting in erasure has declined and then sharply risen in 1988 and 1989. They have declined both as a proportion of cases and of the total number of doctors in the system. By the same token, in 1988 and 1989, twice as many erasures took place as in the two preceding years. This may indicate more serious cases as well as more willingness to be severe than ever before.

Historically, it has mainly been general practitioners who have been referred to the GMC. Hospital doctors have only occasionally reached its disciplinary committee, since there are more local complaint mechanisms through the hospital and district organization. This pattern has been dictated by tradition rather than objectivity. Furthermore, a significant proportion of disciplined GPs are overseas doctors (Rosenthal 1987/1988).

Recent developments in the General Medical Council

The General Medical Council is actively responding to both internal (Robinson 1988) and external criticisms (Smith 1989) about its conduct of disciplinary functions and related matters. It has established an internal working party to discuss adding a new offence: 'serious failure of performance'. The GMC Annual Report for 1989 highlights this effort. This would include clinical competence as well as professional attitude. The internal working party is holding a series of discussions with various branches of the profession. The outcome could be an amendment to the Medical Act. This would reflect a major new and long overdue direction for the GMC.

Another change is that two of the lay members most recently appointed to the GMC are Members of Parliament. This is an idea adapted from the Swedish disciplinary board.

There is also continuing GMC concern with the terminology in its 'Blue Book', *Professional Conduct and Discipline: Fitness to Practise*, particularly the drafting of proscriptions against the 'disparagement' of a colleague. Some doctors have suggested that this constrains them in reporting incompetent colleagues, although senior staff of the GMC note that its original intent was to prevent abuses in pre-NHS competition for patients. The Council is discussing whether to balance this with 'a duty' to report negligent acts.

In the last five years, the number of hospital doctors suspended by their regions in conjunction with possible negligence has risen noticeably. The suspended doctor receives full salary while an official inquiry is conducted, but cannot practise in the region or, for all practical purposes, anywhere else in the National Health Service. Should this trend continue, it can be seen as a functional equivalent of deregistration, an act hitherto the exclusive prerogative of the GMC's Professional Conduct Committee. A new managerial assertiveness may be undercutting the Council's responsibilities with this section of the profession whose practice has not previously been deeply touched by active professional discipline.

THE SWEDISH APPROACH

In Sweden, the body that reviews complaints against doctors is the Medical Responsibility Board (MRB), a federal government agency that functions like an administrative organization (see Table 2.4). The MRB also receives complaints and reviews cases concerning dentists, nurses and other health-related personnel. The Swedish MRB has functioned in its present form for the last ten years. It has evolved through a number of permutations.

History

In 1915 the newly created national Board of Medicine was empowered to both license and discipline district doctors (GPs). After 1947 it took on similar responsibilities for specialists and allied health personnel. When the Board was reorganized in 1968 and became the National Board of Health and Welfare (NBHW) (as it remains today) a separate internal division was created to continue to review complaints against all health practitioners: the Medical Responsibility Board.

Many of the procedural patterns established during this period set the protocols used by the current MRB which became a free-standing govern-

Table 2.4 Swedish Medical Responsibility Board

History	National Board of Health and Welfare committees until 1977 Riksdag Act 1978 created autonomous agency
Composition	4 members of Riksdag 3 union representatives 1 employer representative 1 judge
How financed	Annual budget from government
Types of issue addressed	1 Alleged malpractice 2 General fitness to practise 3 Questions of conscientious care
Who disciplined	Doctors, nurses, dentists, others
Types of action possible	1 No action 2 Admonition 3 Warning 4 Restricted Rights 5 Recall of certificate 6 Re-issue of certificate 7 Referral to courts
Sources of complaints	Individuals (the largest percentage) Hospitals (before 1980) National Board of Health and Welfare Parliamentary ombudsman
How often meet	Once a week in private (approximately 40 weeks a year)
Where meet	In Riksdag committee room
Type of meeting	Resembles administrative court 1 Doctor-reporter presents facts 2 Committee questions, discusses, votes 3 Neither complainant nor accused present
Rights of appeal	Accused and others can appeal

mental body following an Act of 1978. At that time, many Swedish government agencies were reformed to make them more accountable and less bureaucratic. It was also felt that, since the NBHW wrote the health personnel regulations, it should not also judge the abrogation of those regulations.

Composition

Today the MRB is composed of seven members: four members of the Swedish Parliament providing unusually strong consumer representation, a lawyer from the Federation of County Councils (which administer health care facilities) and a representative from each of the three national union conglomerates. The latter include one doctor from the Swedish Medical Association (SMA), one nurse from the Swedish Nurses Association and one representative from an allied health occupation from the Health Aides Association.

The MRB is served by an administrative staff of twenty which includes ten lawyers. It also retains some fifty professional health specialists (doctors, nurses, pharmacists, psychologists, physiotherapists) who serve as the investigators and presenters in cases related to their areas of expertise. Each session of the MRB covers fifteen to twenty-five cases and involves several different presenters. The procedures and regulations it follows are laid out in considerable detail, including the requirement that the Board address every complaint it receives unless the matter is clearly outside its jurisdiction. The meetings of the MRB are held in private without the presence of either the complainant or those complained against.

Influence of the medical profession

An appropriate specialist, matched with the specialty of the doctor involved, researches, writes up and presents each case, with a recommendation for action. The MRB members raise questions from their own point of view. The Members of Parliament are most active, often asking the doctor on the Board to clarify technical, clinical points. Systematic observation of a number of meetings indicates that, although there are only two doctors involved (the presenter and one member), they are disproportionately and consistently influential in decision-making (Rosenthal 1987/1988).

Because both the British and American disciplinary bodies are overwhelmingly dominated by doctors, the Swedish arrangement becomes particularly interesting. It could be argued that the domination of doctors in the first two countries accounts for the pattern found in each: a preponderance of interest in complaints about professional conduct rather than clinical conduct and a great reluctance to impose severe sanctions.

The importance of the presenter can be seen in observations of meetings. For example, the presenter offers rationales for the behaviour of the staff.

> There are shortcomings but we can't accuse the staff; the department was overloaded with work.

The doctor may not have had the correct information but it doesn't matter to the outcomes for the patient. There are so many patients to see.

The presenter, a peer of the accused doctor, is considered to have the necessary technical expertise to evaluate a complaint. There is considerable weight to this logic, and it lies behind the use of a matched specialist to investigate cases, prepare reports and recommend appropriate action. Implicit in the system, however, is the potential for identification with the doctor under review. The importance of medical knowledge to the deliberations of the Board is also reflected in the participation of the physician on the Board. The influence of the physician representing the SMA could be observed in a large number of the cases discussed. He often dominated the discussion (Rosenthal 1987/1988).

The Members of Parliament consistently raised questions from the consumer's point of view but they were only rarely able to bring a majority of the Board to change a recommended action. The most they accomplished was to change the wording or tone of the written report. The presenter's recommendation was sustained in 98 per cent of the cases.

The Swedish disciplinary board might appear to have had significant public representation in its parliamentary members. They are assertive individuals with important influence and status in their own right as elected representatives of the people. They are four out of nine members and are potentially powerful consumer representatives. However, they must still rely on the technical knowledge of the physician presenter and the physician member of the Board. There is a consistent pattern of medical influence on the decision-making process despite the very small number of doctors involved (Rosenthal 1987/1988).

Medical Responsibility Board decision-making

A number of important facts emerge from a study of MRB records that provide insights into patterns of decision-making over the years:

1 The number of complaints is steadily rising.
2 Eighty per cent of the complaints received by the Board concern doctors rather than other health professionals.
3 The number of cases actually taken on by the full Board has been reduced in recent years as a 'preliminary screening' function (like that used by the GMC) has been taken on by the chair of the MRB.
4 The overwhelming majority of cases focus on complaints about alleged diagnostic and therapeutic errors.
5 Most complaints (over 80 per cent) are dismissed. The rest receive either an admonition or a warning. Very few licences are revoked.

6 The number of appeals by both parties has risen in recent years. Just under 10 per cent are successful.

Discussion

The Swedish disciplinary body has taken, as its main interest, the clinical practice behaviour of all personnel. While it takes on and examines other types of complaint, the majority of its caseload concerns alleged malpractice. This is in direct contrast to the British who addressed everything but alleged malpractice, and the USA where clinical competence was not a major concern until recently.

Unlike Britain and the USA, where consumers increasingly take their complaints about doctors to the courts, Swedish consumers can report injuries to a Patient Insurance Fund. Here compensation can be obtained for prescribed categories of injuries without finding a doctor guilty of negligence. This Fund was instituted in 1975. Although injured patients could still go to court, none did until the mid-1980s when a small number of cases were filed. While the introduction of no-fault insurance seems to have temporarily reduced the number of complaints, the MRB is now receiving more complaints, the Patient Insurance Fund office is receiving more claims, and new local county complaints boards are receiving more and more complaints. The latter were instituted in the hope that they would reduce the workload of the MRB by draining away minor complaints. This has not happened.

The number of MRB complaints is high relative to the size of the medical workforce compared to Britain even though, in Sweden, they have not kept pace with the growth in the number of doctors. This may be because Sweden has had few other complaints mechanisms or because the country has high doctor/population and bed/population ratios, and a high hospital admissions rate (see Tables 2.5–2.7).

The MRB is, of course, assisted by an administrative staff which serves as a gatekeeper to the system. The chair of the MRB reviews all complaints but only dismisses those where the MRB is the wrong authority or where a two-year time limit has elapsed. The number of cases completed, however, is correlated with the number of staff available to process them and the amount of time devoted to the task of review by the MRB itself. This means a rising backlog of cases carried over from year to year. The average duration of a case from filing to disposition is now one year. This indicates why the number of cases, over the years, is relatively static. Resources limit what can be done, as noted in Britain.

The MRB imposes its most severe sanction sparingly, particularly on doctors. Doctors are the most likely subjects of complaints because their role in medical care is the most visible and they take the most responsibility. It is also possible that only the more serious complaints against nurses and dentists are taken on while trivial complaints against doctors continue to be included in the caseload of the MRB for public relations purposes. By comparison with doctors, dentists are seven times more likely, and nurses six and a half times more likely, to have their licences revoked (Rosenthal 1987/1988).

Recent developments in Sweden

In 1989 a government commission reviewing the MRB, found little to change. As has been mentioned, the chair now acts as a 'screener' for all the complaints received and disposes of a number of minor complaints himself without passing them on as cases to the Board. This has reduced the number of cases that the full MRB reviews. The staff has been increased somewhat to try to reduce the backlog of cases. The MRB used to publish a quarterly review of its cases for the benefit of the medical profession. As a cost-saving measure, this has been reduced to an annual compendium although selected cases are still published periodically in the *Swedish Medical Journal.*

COMPARING THE THREE DISCIPLINARY BODIES

The British General Medical Council disciplinary committees, the Swedish Medical Responsibility Board and the American state medical boards, as represented by the state of Michigan can be compared and contrasted in a variety of ways. Material from this study has focused on organizational characteristics, disciplinary concerns and selected patterns of decision-making.

Organizational characteristics

The most important difference between the disciplinary boards is their composition. The British and American boards are dominated by doctors, although the American boards are in the public sector as state administrative agencies. The Swedish board is also a public administrative agency but only has one doctor on it. Research indicates, however, that this single doctor exercises great influence.

The British GMC is unique in being a medical professional body, created by parliamentary statute but controlled by the profession itself. In Johnson's (1981) terms, it is an example of 'collegial' regulation, while the Swedish and American bodies, part of the array of government structure, are 'mediative'. That is, the state plays the role of a mediator between the profession and the public. None the less, these organizations cannot function without the knowledge that the medical profession possesses so doctors continue to have a dominant influence even where their numbers are small.

The British and American boards operate using legal models, particularly with reference to a form of 'due process'. Swedish hearings are more like a formal meeting although the MRB itself is carefully regulated. Each board can take a similar range of actions. All three have only recently begun to develop separate approaches for impaired doctors.

Disciplinary issues

The most interesting difference between the boards is the disciplinary issues on which each has chosen to dwell. For the British GMC this has been primarily professional conduct; until recently this has also been the case for the American boards. Mounting public pressure is now shifting more attention to clinical conduct, particularly in the USA but also to some extent in Britain. This has been the emphasis in Sweden for a considerable time (see Table 2.5). What might account for these differences?

The answer to this important question is multi-faceted. It is likely that doctors are reluctant to criticize each other for reasons of professional collegiality. They also share convictions about the ambiguities of medical practice and what the profession widely calls 'unanticipated complications and clinical uncertainty'. These are transcultural characteristics shared by medical professions in many societies.

All this is changing now, particularly in Britain where the use of the courts for medical injury has risen dramatically. Even Sweden has experienced a small number of medical injury court cases recently. In the United States public discussion periodically escalates about these issues. The disciplinary bodies have been under pressure to act more rigorously with reference to clinical competence and negligence.

In Britain, general practitioners have been the specialty of major interest to the GMC disciplinary process. Why? 'Tradition' appears to be the answer. In Sweden, too, it was GPs who were historically disciplined by the bureaucratic mechanisms with the Medical Society having responsibility for specialists, but this changed by 1947. The typical doctor complained against to the Swedish MRB is now, however, a surgeon. Statistics on this subject have not been kept by the State of Michigan Board.

Table 2.5 Nature of the cases reviewed: Michigan, USA, Britain and Sweden

Michigan, USA		Britain		Sweden	
Nature of cases reviewed	1984–85* (%)	Nature of cases reviewed	1971 and 1981 (%)	Nature of cases reviewed	1973 and 1981 (%)
Negligence, incompetence	33	Neglect of professional responsibility	7.0	Diagnostic errors	26.6
Professional misconduct	14	Personal conduct derogatory to reputation of the profession	61.8	Treatment errors	39.2
				General behaviour	26.6
		Abuse of professional privileges	15.8		
Criminal behaviour	20			Mistakes in practical procedures	17.7
Impairment	6			Doctor's certification of patient illness	17.5
Drug dealing	15			Wrong/delayed information	10.2
		Canvassing	5.4		
Other	10	Other	7.5		

* Earliest data available

Note: The author takes responsibility for categorization of cases.

Sources: Michigan, USA: State of Michigan Department of Licensing and Regulation, 1990.
Britain: GMC Annual Reports, 1973 and 1981.
Sweden: MRB files: random sample of cases, 1971 and 1981.

Table 2.6 Complaints as a proportion of doctors: three-country comparison

Year	Michigan, USA			Britain			Sweden		
	Number of doctors*	Number of complaints received	Complaint/ doctor ratio	Number of doctors	Number of complaints received†	Complaint/ doctor ratio	Number of doctors	Number of complaints received	Complaint/ doctor ratio
1974				47,795	847	1:56	13,260	704	1:19
1975				49,299	888	1:55	13,750	658	1:20
1976				50,270	930	1:54	14,450	602	1:24
1977				51,416	896	1:57	15,410	573	1:26
1978				56,141	884	1:63	16,340	616	1:26
1979				57,640	920	1:62	16,800	621	1:27
1980				59,433	924	1:66	16,900	648	1:26
1981	23,996	363	1:66	60,835	935	1:65	17,400	564	1:31
1982	24,619	292	1:84				18,400	680	1:27
1983	24,755	398	1:62				21,671	683	1:32
1984	25,574	362	1:70				22,771	790	1:29
1985	26,083	300	1:87						
1986	26,753	343	1:78						
1987	26,387	618	1:42						
1988	28,170								
Average (7-year)			1:69	Average (8-year)		1:59	Average (11-year)		1:26

* Michigan, USA includes both MDs and DOs (Doctors of Osteopathy) licensed to practise
† Proportion concerning doctors

Sources: Michigan, USA: State of Michigan Department of Licensing and Regulation, 1990.
Britain: Health and Personal Social Service Statistics for England, 1974–80. GMC Annual Reports, 1974–84.
Sweden: MRB files, 1974–84; manpower statistics from the National Board of Health and Welfare.

Complaints rising everywhere

Complaints are rising in all three countries (see Table 2.6). This seems most likely to be a reflection of heightened consumer awareness and education as well as a general lowering of trust for authority. It is particularly interesting to look at the comparative figures for the number of complaints as a proportion of doctors and the number of licences withdrawn as a proportion of doctors. The latter might be seen as a measure of willingness to impose the most severe sanctions.

Licence withdrawal as a proportion of doctors

The British revoke considerably fewer licences than either the American or Swedish boards (see Table 2.7). The complaint/doctor ratio is highest in Sweden but this may be explained by the lack of other complaint mechanisms. The American ratio may be related to the fact that Americans are

Table 2.7 Number of licences taken away: three-country comparison

Year	Michigan, USA	Britain	Sweden
1973		1: 4,675	1:1,261
1974		1: 3,677	1:4,420
1975		1: 2,348	1:2,750
1976		1: 4,189	1:4,817
1977		1: 7,306	1:3,853
1978		1: 5,103	1:2,723
1979		1: 5,240	1:2,800
1980	1:5,803	1:11,887	1:2,817
1981	1:5,999		
1982	1:3,517		
1983	1:2,250		
1984	1:2,841		
1985	1:4,347		
1986	1:2,972	1:10,472	
1987	1:3,769	1: 9,038	
Average	1:3,937	1: 8,354	1:3,180

Sources: Government manpower statistics, General Medical Council and Medical Responsibility Board reports and files; State of Michigan Department of Licensing and Regulation.

more likely to turn to their lawyers than to their disciplinary boards. As for the British GMC erasing proportionately fewer doctors from the Register, this may be a function of the GMC's 'collegial' nature. This is an important issue requiring more research and analysis.

CONCLUSIONS

Studies of these disciplinary bodies suggest that what they can accomplish is limited for a wide variety of reasons. They are seriously constrained by limited resources. There is little documented relationship between their work and the general incidence of medical injury, let alone injury caused by incompetent doctors. There is no evidence that they act as a deterrent to either unprofessional or poor clinical behaviour. They can only function as one small element within what must be a larger, much more complex set of mechanisms to deal with incompetence, injury and redress for the patient. These mechanisms are likely to include systematic peer review, medical audit, risk management, useful continuing medical education, information feedback, evaluation, and powerful structural and financial incentives to improve the quality of medical care.

This does not mean that disciplinary bodies are not necessary or that they cannot be improved. They need to be studied and understood as they function today. They need to have more clearly defined tasks, perhaps to focus on the impaired or criminal doctor, and to do this more effectively. They need better resources and training. And it needs to be understood that they are not necessarily effective mechanisms for identifying, helping or sanctioning the chronically or episodically incompetent doctor. They are only one part of the larger and more complex effort that must be mounted.

3 Complaining – what's the use?

Linda Mulcahy and Sally Lloyd-Bostock

Quality in health care has traditionally been defined by providers with reference to technical criteria. In recent years we have witnessed an emerging interest in the notion of quality assurance as a means of reducing the possibility of mishaps or mistakes occurring.[1] Concern for quality does not just relate to the appropriateness and effectiveness of clinical procedures, but extends to all aspects of the services provided by medical staff and administrators, and to the process of care viewed from the patient's perspective.

It has, then, become fashionable to weave patient evaluations of care into the quality formula. The stimulus in Britain can be traced to the publication in 1983 of the report of the inquiry by Sir Roy Griffiths into National Health Service management, which generated considerable interest in notions of 'patient satisfaction' and 'quality of care', themes which were subsequently reiterated in the Conservative government's White Paper, *Working for Patients* (1989).[2] In a letter to the Secretary of State, Griffiths (1983) asserted that:

> it is central to the approach of management, in planning and delivering services . . . to ascertain how well the service is being delivered at local level by obtaining the experience and perceptions of patients and the community.

Evaluation of care by users of the service can take a number of forms: patient satisfaction surveys; choice of hospital or clinician; responses to hospital charges; malpractice claims and complaints about hospital services. This chapter focuses specifically on one of the indicators being used in some quality assurance programmes: the hospital complaint. The issue it addresses is the extent to which complaints can contribute to the specification, attainment and assessment of quality.

Our discussion draws on research being conducted at the Centre for Socio-Legal Studies, University of Oxford, on the operation of the hospital complaints machinery in England and Wales.[3] The chapter is organised in two parts. The first part outlines the National Health Service complaints procedure in operation in England and Wales and discusses its strengths and weaknesses for quality assurance purposes. Our comments on the present system seek to highlight the factors which policy-makers need to take into account in designing a system geared towards quality assurance. The second part of the chapter attempts to clarify the uses that can and cannot be made of complaints, taking into account the social psychological dynamics of complaining.

COMPLAINTS AND THE QUALITY ASSURANCE ARGUMENT

We do not question the proposition that users' assessments should form part of any quality formula. Service users' knowledge is privileged. Patients may be the only ones who know that a doctor has made a mistake; that they are still in pain; that their lunch is cold; that they were not bathed on the previous day. But complaints are not received solely from patients. Friends, relatives and pressure groups may also have cause to complain either on their own behalf or that of a patient.[4] Their assessments of hospital services are as valuable. Friends or relatives may be the only ones who know the true extent to which a patient's condition has deteriorated; that a nurse has been rude; that inadequate notice has been given of a patient's arrival home; that the seats in the waiting room are uncomfortable; that the car park is always full. Both groups have a unique perspective on the service delivery process.[5] They are able to tell managers and clinicians things which they cannot always anticipate or learn from other sources. It seems obvious that one way of taking account of users' perceptions and knowledge is to pay attention to complaints. Information on expressed dissatisfaction in the health service provides data on the consequences of poor quality which can be used to highlight bad processes and outcomes.

Drummond and Morgan (1988) have argued that, viewed in this way, complaints can provide a stimulus in service delivery, a vehicle for developing staff and an opportunity to educate service providers. Most important, they believe that complaints facilitate consideration of whether the mishap, misdeed, accident or misunderstanding could have been avoided and whether a change in procedure is required. They have labelled this the *learning approach*:

> data on complaints may guide the priorities of the quality assurance or consumer affairs department . . . A rise in the number of complaints in a given area may suggest that a more systematic survey on consumer satisfaction be mounted or that extra in-service training be given. It

might signal a fundamental deficiency in working practices or resource provision which should be considered further. In essence complaints and other comments on service delivery should be viewed as an important source of information on consumer satisfaction and service standards which could be considered alongside other information in the interests of improving service quality.

(Drummond and Morgan 1988: 16)

The quality assurance rhetoric is attractive, the temptation to build complaints into a quality formula almost irresistible. They represent free feedback which is available regardless of hospital initiatives or levels of funding. The reality is rather more complicated. To what extent can complaints provide useful indicators of areas where resources should be allocated or practices changed?

The science of using complaints in this way has to be exact and its limitations recognized. Managers need to be clear about the types of system which are able to capture complaints that can be of value for quality assurance purposes and the ways in which the system's design influences the nature of the information received. They must be able to assess the weight to be attached to each available item of information. How many complaints about the rude demeanour of a clinician need to be registered, for instance, before it is appropriate to raise the matter with him or her and to press for a change in behaviour? What other data need to be used in conjunction with that extracted from complaints to substantiate claims made by service users? In deciding what weight to attribute to the information available we need to understand more about the dynamics of complaining behaviour. Who makes complaints and why? Who does *not* complain? Are there treatment episodes which are more likely to prompt dissatisfaction?

THE NATIONAL HEALTH SERVICE HOSPITAL COMPLAINTS SYSTEM

As described in official documents, the National Health Service hospital complaints machinery appears to have two principal aims. First, it seeks to provide responses to and redress of citizen grievances. Second, and more important for present purposes, it seeks to encourage the managerial monitoring of adverse incidents and revision of practice or policy in response to them.

The current system is governed by the Hospital Complaints Act 1985 and guidance issued under it. Under the Act health authorities are *obliged,* for the first time, to establish a formal complaints procedure. The most recent guidelines are contained in a 1988 Circular, HC(88)37. This sets out a general principle that constructive criticisms can be valuable managerial tools. More specifically it requires health authorities to publicize their complaints machinery and 'monitor' complaints received. Each NHS unit[6] must appoint a *designated officer* in charge of handling complaints. This officer will investigate and respond to any complaint classified as *formal*. A formal complaint is defined as one which cannot be dealt with informally at ward level; which is of such concern to the patient that it warrants further consideration and a formal response by a senior officer; or one which the complainant feels he or she cannot address directly to the staff involved. Anonymized reports on each complaint are forwarded for monitoring purposes via the District General Manager to the health authority, which also receives quarterly reports on outstanding cases.

If complainants are dissatisfied with the way the designated officer has responded to their complaint they can do one of two things, depending on whether or not their dissatisfaction relates to clinical matters. First, if the complaint concerns clinical aspects of care, they can refer the matter to the Regional Medical Officer who is expected to arrange a meeting between the complainant and the medical staff involved. Where the complaint remains unresolved the Regional Medical Officer can consider sending the matter to an independent professional review. The aim of this procedure is for clinicians to assess whether the clinical judgement of a colleague has been exercised appropriately.[7] The reviewers are two independent consultants appointed by the Joint Consultative Committee who have volunteered to sit on the case. Second, where complainants are dissatisfied with the way the health authority has handled the investigation and the response to their complaint they can refer the matter to the Health Service Commissioner who has the power, where seen fit, to initiate a full inquiry into the manner in which the complaint has been handled.

Subject matter and number of complaints received

Complaints about NHS hospitals cover a wide range of topics from allegations of mismanaged births through concerns about the abrupt behaviour of a member of staff to complaints about dust under a hospital bed or the size of a boiled egg served for breakfast. Over a three-month period, one of the units co-operating in our study received formal complaints about closure of a ward; rude staff; missing flowers; waiting time at out-patients; lack of funding for specialist operations; failure to treat because of the breakdown of machinery; inadequate after-care arrangements made on discharge; lazy staff; failure of an ambulance to turn up; length of hospital waiting lists;

reduction of services because of cuts; charges made for contact lens solution; unavailability of funding for pioneering operations; and blindness allegedly caused by the negligence of unit doctors.

Official statistics from the Department of Health divide complaints into two main categories: clinical and non-clinical. About 40 per cent of all complaints fell into the former category throughout the 1980s. The volume of complaints received by hospitals in England and Wales has increased substantially since statistics were first compiled. The number of hospital complaints almost doubled from 15,112 in 1977 to 29,596 in 1987–88. This did not simply reflect an increase in the volume of activity: the number of hospital complaints per thousand in-patients and day cases increased from 2.6 in 1977 to 4.0 in 1987–88.

HOW EFFECTIVE IS THE MACHINERY?

Hospital complaints systems can aim to achieve a number of goals. They can provide a forum for users of the services to express their anxieties; facilitate the accountability of managers and health care professionals; prompt redress, explanations or compensation; form part of a public relations exercise; act as a filter or buffer for more serious allegations; provide an alternative to litigation, and provide valuable information about administrative and medical mishaps for quality assurance purposes. Not all these aims are compatible. A system which seeks to ward off potential litigation may not, for example, be easily reconciled with the provision of a frank and satisfying explanation of a mishap to a complainant. In designing and implementing a complaints system, choices have to be made as to which of various competing aims is to be given priority.

If complaints are to be of use in a quality assurance system, three basic priorities have to be recognized. First, if maximum use is to be made of the information available from complaints, complaints must be encouraged. Only then can managers begin to claim that their priority is to obtain the fullest information possible about the failings of the system. The second requirement of a successful quality assurance programme is that it should be integrated and hospital-wide. There must be a free flow of information internally, so that those responsible for the assessment and monitoring of complaints can be provided with all the information available about the nature of the complaint. The third is that statistics used to monitor performance over time must be designed with a quality assurance motive in mind. The guidance currently in force fails to satisfy any of these criteria fully.

Encouraging complaints – the proactive approach

It is clear that, for reasons we discuss below, voiced grievances are not representative of all dissatisfaction with hospital services. One way to mitigate the problems caused by relying on so unrepresentative a sample is to encourage complaints, to adopt a proactive approach. The National Association of Health Authorities has argued that encouraging complaints is a risk worth taking if quality is to be achieved.[8] However, the current system does little to welcome complaints. Among other things guidelines require that information about how to complain is not to be displayed in hospital wards in case it prompts patients to make 'unfounded' or 'frivolous' complaints. As long ago as 1973 the Davies Committee on Hospital Complaints[9] recognized that:

> If patients are to make full use of procedures for making suggestions and complaints they must be told about them and helped to operate them. Research and other evidence shows that patients do not usually know how to make complaints, sometimes because they are not told at all and sometimes because reluctance to encourage complaints makes the message obscure.
>
> (Department of Health and Social Security 1973: 39)

There are a number of indications that the system has changed little since then. The Association of Community Health Councils has claimed that, in its members' experience, few health authorities are fully meeting their obligations under current guidelines to publicize their complaints procedures (ACHCEW 1990). Instead of producing special leaflets encouraging feedback, many are said to rely on sections inserted into pre-existing patient information booklets. This not only makes the information less accessible, but it also means that those using out-patients, accident and emergency, and long-term residential care tend not to receive it. Prescott-Clarke *et al.* (1988) found in a survey of patients in four health districts that only 5 per cent of those questioned knew how to make a formal complaint. Another survey of 650 individuals in a Midlands town in 1987 revealed that only 8 per cent of interviewees claimed to know how to make a complaint. Fifty per cent knew of the existence of the Community Health Council but less than 20 per cent knew what they did (*Health Service Journal*, May 1987, 614).[10]

The problems of knowing how to complain are compounded by the complexity of current procedures. Alongside the hospital complaints procedure already described, we find a separate system for complaints relating to general practitioners, dentists, opticians and pharmacists administered by the Family Practitioner Committee (now the Family Health

Services Authority). If a complaint involves an allegation of serious profes-
sional misconduct by a doctor, it can be referred to the General Medical
Council. Similar complaints against nurses are dealt with by the United
Kingdom Central Council for Nursing, Midwifery and Health Visiting.
Complaints about special hospitals must be referred to the Parliamentary
Commissioner for Administration unless they concern the exercise of ex-
ecutive powers, in which case they must be referred to the Home Secretary.

The various procedures have different aims and there is at present no
single body capable of handling a multi-dimensional complaint, although
some informal cross-referencing may be done by Community Health
Councils. Little attempt has been made to promote collaboration[11] and not
all complaints fit neatly into just one jurisdiction. The jurisdictional diver-
gence according to whether a hospital complaint is of a clinical or non-
clinical nature is particularly artificial: in 1985–86, for instance, the Health
Service Commissioner completed 131 investigations but was unable to
consider another 131 applications because they involved an element of
clinical judgement and thus fell outside his jurisdiction. Reforms giving
managers a pivotal role in both cases have long been called for.[12] It is easy
to recognize that the resources and stamina of many complainants are
exhausted through having approached the wrong channel. In the words of
one critic:

> The process for airing grievances, investigating complaints and pro-
> viding explanations when things go wrong are considered by those who
> use them to be long winded, cumbersome, bureaucratic and strongly
> weighted in favour of the medical profession.
>
> (ACHCEW 1990: 2)

In addition to the problems of knowing how and where to complain, much
has been made in the literature of complainants' fears of victimization. The
theme was particularly prevalent during the 1960s when a number of
government reports highlighted the need for a complaints procedure which
was alert to this problem. The Davies Committee found that particular
problems arose when encouraging staff to complain either on a patient's or
on their own behalf. Staff were often reluctant to criticize colleagues for
fear of internal retribution. The same fear often prevented patients, their
relatives or friends from making a complaint, particularly where the patient
was living indefinitely in hospital.

The managerial role in quality assurance programmes

The second requirement of a successful quality assurance programme is
that those responsible for the assessment and monitoring of complaints

must be provided with all the information available about the substance of complaints. Good sense suggests that this should be the domain of management, occupying, as they do, a more independent standpoint than staff who are involved in the direct delivery of services. In our analysis of health authority files, however, we have discovered little evidence to date of health authority officers following up complaints. There have been no instances, for example, of designated officers asking the most obvious source, the complainant, for further information. This is despite the fact that many letters of complaint contain little detail about the alleged event or circumstance complained of.[13] Moreover, most cases prompt no further action by the authority once a letter of reply has been sent. The finding suggests that rather than valuing the information provided, managers place greater priority on processing complaints as quickly as possible. In the words of one manager:

> Looking back, I wonder if I could/should have done more personally on the investigative side. The handling of complaints is only ever a part of anyone's job (there are always competing demands on time), and it may be tempting to rely too much on written communications – which can usually be patched together to make an 'acceptable' reply – rather than going out and discussing the matter with the staff most closely involved.
>
> (Truelove 1985: 230)

Particular problems arise in the supervision of complaints relating to clinical aspects of care. While current guidance appears to allocate overall responsibility for the handling of complaints to a 'designated officer' it allows clinicians to take over the handling of complaints relating to clinical judgement. The authority for this compromise derives from an agreement made between the Department of Health and Social Security and the medical profession which was set out in the 1981 circular HC(81)5. This allows the consultant in charge of a case to respond directly to the complainant on the clinical aspects of a complaint. Where the clinician receives the complaint direct, it need not be referred to or discussed with the designated complaints officer. Any reference to clinical matters in a reply by an administrator, however, must first be referred to the clinician involved for approval.

This undermining of managerial responsibility is exacerbated if the complainant is dissatisfied with the first response and decides to refer the matter to the clinical review procedure explained above. A referral of this kind effectively takes the matter completely out of the managerial sphere and into a formal medical self-regulatory mechanism which offers minimal feedback to managers. Although the district administrator will write to the complainant on completion of the review, the terms of the letter will be directed by the Regional Medical Officer and the administrator is unlikely to have had any personal involvement with the review. The Regional Medical Officer is not obliged to take any action on the recommendations of the reviewers and there is no guidance on the form which the reviewers' report should take. Neither is there a requirement that managers other than the Regional Medical Officer be informed of the results or any formal procedure to ensure that proposals have been acted upon.

The appeal system does perform some quality assurance functions. The Department of Health and Social Security reported in 1983 that a number of improvements had been made to services as a result of the clinical reviews.[14] Examples included the urgent centralization of a city's renal services in a single purpose-built department, improved ante-natal monitoring procedures and improved clinical record-keeping.[15] But the difficulty is that the reviews are not part of a fully integrated centralized programme. This is of particular concern since the cases are often the most serious in terms of severity of harm and potential legal liability and warrant in-depth consideration by all involved in reviews of care. The design of the system clearly fails to facilitate this goal, limiting the free flow of information to quality managers.

The use of statistics

The proactive approach also requires that reliable statistics be kept for the purposes of maintaining a global perspective on complaints and facilitating comparisons between districts. At present, officers are required to monitor complaints at a local level and take appropriate action where necessary. The value of such exercises is questionable. We have already suggested that voiced grievances do not represent the true level of dissatisfaction. Little can be learnt about a global perspective from the bare statistical returns which are sent to district health authorities and ultimately to the Department of Health. Returns to the Department do little more than classify complaints received according to whether they are wholly or partly clinical, concern community or hospital services and how they have been investigated. The preliminary findings of our own study suggest that the classification according to whether the complaint is wholly or partly clinical or not is particularly unreliable. Apart from the fact that many grievances contain both clinical and non-clinical elements, many letters of complaint contain more than one allegation. Under the current recording system this makes accurate records impossible. Moreover, staff clearly have difficulty in discerning what is clinical. Complaints about doctors' attitudes are, for instance, variously included in either category.

In addition, although the guidance allows oral as well as written complaints to be dealt with in the complaints machinery, it cannot deal with *informal* complaints. Governing guidance encourages the informal resolution of such disputes where possible but does not require that the details of informal complaints be recorded. Little is known of how staff at ward level use their discretion in steering a complaint towards formal or informal channels, but it may well be that in a system which does not reward proactive behaviour in response to complaints the incentive weighs heavily on the side of informality. In a reactive environment complaints are easily viewed by ward staff as mere criticism.

THE DYNAMICS OF COMPLAINING

So far we have been considering ways in which the design and operation of a hospital complaints system may limit the information about dissatisfaction that it generates. It is equally important to consider the psychological and social nature of complaining itself, irrespective of the particular complaints system. Who complains to hospitals, and why? How does the 'complaining' population relate to the broader population of patients and other health service users? To what extent are matters complained about representative of the causes of dissatisfaction among users of the health service? How do events complained about relate to the population of adverse events that might indicate failures in standards of quality? These questions are central to an understanding of the ways in which complaints can and cannot be used for quality assurance purposes. It cannot be assumed that if the quality of service is inadequate then consumer dissatisfaction with the service will become evident as long as the machinery for expression of the dissatisfaction is available.[16]

A number of studies have attempted to estimate the number of adverse occurrences, or adverse consequences of treatment arising in hospitals, regardless of whether a claim or complaint has been lodged.[17] It is clear that mishaps identified in complaints are only a small minority of adverse occurrences. No matter how much complaints were encouraged, some incidents would never come to light for the simple reason that service users are unaware of them. Patients and their relatives quite often do not know that something has gone wrong, perhaps because they were absent, unconscious, delirious or confused at the time, or because they do not have the technical skill to recognize that an adverse incident has occurred. But even where the patient or other service user is aware of, and dissatisfied about, an adverse occurrence, there are still many reasons why complaints received should be treated as a very incomplete picture of dissatisfaction felt.

Who complains?

Hospital staff responsible for handling complaints to whom we have spoken, in both Britain and the US, are aware that complainants and the matters they complain about are unrepresentative. A member of hospital staff in California said in interview:

> Sure we get patients who complain but they are not representative. If you took fifteen patients a week in a totally arbitrary sample, marched them into the hospital director's room and grilled them about their hospital experience you would probably get a lot more valuable information than from someone who had an axe to grind. Apart from anything else the person who makes the complaint has an incentive to beef it up.

In the experience of one complaints officer in Britain, the propensity to complain and styles of complaining vary according to the individual:

> Some people complain only reluctantly and as a last resort, when prompted by deep emotion. Some complain reasonably on reasonable grounds. Some complain unreasonably on reasonable grounds. Some complain reasonably on unreasonable grounds. A few . . . complain unreasonably on unreasonable grounds. A few seem to be 'born complainants' who relish a battle and will complain on any grounds whatsoever.
>
> (Truelove 1985: 229)

The tendency to complain has been studied in a range of different settings. The literature links the likelihood of complaining to a range of personal characteristics – class and socio-economic status (Ross and Littlefield [1978]; Best and Andreasen [1976]; Vidmar [1981]; Hunting and Neuwith [1962]; Wheeler *et al.* [1987]; Best [1981]); sex (Black [1976]; Felstiner *et al.* [1980–81]; Doherty [1977]); age (Felstiner *et al.* [1980–81]; Doherty and Haven [1977]; Hunting and Neuwith [1962]; McNeil *et al.* [1979]; Griffiths [1977]); self-perception and attitudes (Addiss [1980]; Steele [1977]); knowledge (Galanter [1974]; Galanter [1976]); education (Addiss [1980]; Felstiner *et al.* [1980–81]; Hunting and Neuwith [1962]); religion (Greenhouse [1986] in which the religious doctrine of Baptists is examined as a means of understanding their ethics of avoidance); race and political views (Black [1973]; Felstiner *et al.* [1980–81]; Nader [1980]). The literature emphasizes feelings of helplessness and fatalism, a power–impotence dimension. In a health care setting, patients may feel powerless, and value may be placed on the 'good patient' who is compliant, does what he or she is told, does not question and is deferential. Patients with a handicap or disability may feel particularly vulnerable (Stacey 1976).

However worthy of complaint an incident may be, it must be remembered that complaining can be emotionally and socially costly to the complainant. People generally avoid overt disputes within continuing relationships, and may therefore be less inclined to complain to a hospital if their treatment is not complete. For some people the anticipated distress alone may be enough to discourage embarking on a dispute. People differ in their perceptions of what is complaint-worthy, and in how much they will tolerate without complaining. Thresholds of tolerance may be determined by many factors including personal characteristics, prior expectations of the service,[18] and the amount of previous contact with the hospital. Moreover, thresholds differ according to the circumstances. Laura Nader recounts the story of a time-conscious airline passenger who made no objection when a steward spilt coffee and orange juice on him:

> Yes, I complain when something causes me to lose time. Time is all I've got. When a 'phone company overbills and I have to cross the city to get it straightened out, that makes me angry and I complain. But right now I'm just sitting here goin' nowhere; my suit is dirty and needs cleaning anyway, and mistakes do happen.
>
> (Nader 1980: 8)

The Institute for Operational Research conducted its own research for the Davies Committee on Hospital Complaints into dissatisfaction with hospitals and how dissatisfaction related to complaining. Of those in-patients interviewed who were dissatisfied with the service they had received, but had *not* complained, 33 per cent considered that the matter was not important enough; 21 per cent felt that there was no point in complaining as no action would be taken anyway; 20 per cent said they had consideration for others and could understand the problems faced by staff; 9 per cent said that they did not have the nerve to complain; 8 per cent said that initial anxiety had been overcome; 7 per cent said that they were too lazy to complain; and 6 per cent said that they did not think about it at the time.

If complainants could be characterized in more detail, it might theoretically be possible to weight information gleaned from complaints to take some account of the tendency of certain groups to complain more readily than others. Our current project will produce fuller data on the characteristics of hospital complainants.

Alternatives to making a formal complaint

When health service users do voice dissatisfaction it cannot be assumed that they will do so through the formal complaints machinery, and therefore be represented in official statistics or health authority files. A number of alternative channels exist: family, friends, neighbours, colleagues, community medical staff, pressure groups, community health councils. In their research into dissatisfied patients in North America, May and Stengel (1990) discovered that a host of informal mechanisms for the expression of grievance attract complainants long before formal channels would do so. The most common was the 'defiant' act of changing doctors. Similarly, one inner city district health authority in our current study found that complaints about ethnic issues were more likely to be voiced in the office of the newly appointed ethnic welfare officer than through the formal machinery.

It is recognized in the literature on disputing that the audience initially chosen for the expression of a grievance plays an important role in any subsequent development of the dispute, affecting resolution choices and the likelihood of the grievance being formally expressed. Audiences help to define the experience and can encourage or discourage further voicing (May [1990]; Harris *et al.* [1984]; Hunting and Neuwith [1962]; Felstiner *et al.* [1980–81]). Some audiences for complaints, such as community health councils, are clearly in a better position than others to suggest appropriate formal channels of complaint. Patients who 'lump it' are less likely to indicate they knew who to talk to.

What do complainants want?

What do people achieve, or hope to achieve, by complaining? It tends to be assumed that when people complain they do so in order to achieve some further goal – getting matters corrected, obtaining an explanation or apology, perhaps obtaining compensation. However, it is also recognised that complaining can be an end in itself. Thus, Margaret Stacey writes, 'The tales which laymen tell each other about difficulties and indignities encountered seem to act as a safety valve or to be a way of sharing comfort rather than providing a "charter for action"' (Stacey 1976: 199).

People's motives in complaining are not well understood, but they are fundamental to an understanding of who complains and why. Our current research aims to shed some light on the matter by interviewing complainants, and by studying letters of complaint. Complaints vary enormously, and it will not be possible to generalize about reasons for complaining. But it is already clear that to think of complaints as a means towards a further goal is too simple. For many complaints there is little evidence that complainants have a clearly formulated goal when they initially complain, though they may develop clear goals if the complaint is carried to further stages. It is comparatively rare for complainants actually to ask for anything, even an explanation, in a letter of complaint. It is probable that some complaints to hospitals are better seen as ends in themselves than as instrumental or goal directed. Where the complainant does 'want something' it may well be an appropriate *social* response to the complaint. Making a complaint can be seen as initiating a social sequence in which the hospital is called to account, and is expected to respond accordingly.

What do they complain about?

If complainants are unrepresentative, what about the matters they complain about? If complaint-worthy events are experienced randomly by individuals prone or not prone to complain, perhaps those events will be randomly sampled in complaints. We have already mentioned that certain incidents could never come to light through complaints because potential complainants do not know about them. But even among the rest, it cannot be assumed that the subject matter of complaints is representative of areas of dissatisfaction. Nor can it be assumed that expressed dissatisfaction identifies a failure in quality.

It appears from our data so far that complainants tend to complain about some things and not others. One might expect that matters complained about would be the more 'serious' causes for concern, but that is not necessarily the case. For example, many complaints concern housekeeping matters, being kept waiting, or problems over hospital transport. It may be that dissatisfied patients complain about these matters because they feel on safer ground than if complaining about clinical judgement. One complainant in our study expressed concern about the 'hotel services' provided to her husband in the last days of his life. She complained that his bed linen was not clean; that his hair was not washed; that his food was cold. A meeting was arranged so that she could discuss the issue with the health authority staff involved. The minutes of the meeting reveal that the complainant's more important concerns were that her husband's illness had gone undiagnosed until it was too late and that earlier intervention by medical staff would have saved his life.

Other complaints are much more general statements of problems and difficulties with life rather than specific complaints or criticisms. For example:

> Here I am with my pension nearly cut in half with the same bills to pay as well as having to keep buying more and more clothes for my wife. Her clothes having to be in the wash as well as getting torn trying to get them on her.

Or again:

It has made me a widow and I am broken hearted and this treatment that he had in the last weeks of his life does not make me feel any better . . . the dirty dinner dishes well into the afternoon . . . I was tired when I got home, after all I am 67 and did the journey too.

Certain clusters of complaint seem likely to warrant special attention. One is complaints following a death. Some types of treatment seem particularly likely to give rise to complaints – for example, specialties where anxieties and emotions are more likely to run high, or where the expectations of satisfaction are particularly strong, such as obstetrics.

We have raised more questions than we have answered about the dynamics of complaining: our current research will provide more information on some of them. Our point, however, is that if complaints are to be used for quality assurance purposes, not only do we need a complaints system designed to that end, we also need to understand the dynamics of complaining. Complaints cannot be looked on as straightforward representative indicators of dissatisfaction. This does not necessarily undermine the importance of what the complainant has to say but rather acknowledges that evaluations can adopt a peculiar form when expressed as complaints. It is questionable whether, under any complaints system, complaints could be reliable indicators either of the extent of felt dissatisfaction or of the matters that give rise to this.

CONCLUSION

Complaints generate large quantities of information which appear to be relevant to the issue of quality assurance. We have argued that the contribution which they can make is not simple or straightforward. Our analysis of existing hospital complaints procedures shows that the information on dissatisfaction available through complaints is extremely unrepresentative. They cannot be looked on as directly representative of levels of dissatisfaction or adverse events. Under any complaints system, the social and psychological nature of complaining limits the uses that can be made of complaints to assess or re-define quality. In addition, the system in operation in England and Wales is not designed to facilitate optimum use of the information available. To be of maximum use for quality assurance purposes, complaints must be encouraged. While in no way suggesting that complaints should be ignored, we argue that the goals of quality assurance and monitoring of standards are not compatible with other potential goals of a complaints procedure, such as satisfying complainants or minimizing negligence claims.

Discussion of the role of complaints in quality assurance has to be seen in the context of current debate about reforms and quality in the health service. The present government is placing increasing emphasis not just on cost containment but on achieving value for money. It has argued that it is the way in which the service is managed rather than the levels of funding which is causing problems. Managers and clinicians are under pressure to develop quality assurance programmes which foster greater accountability. However, the concept of quality assurance is not easy to grapple with nor is its implementation cheap. It is clear that a concept as elusive as 'quality' in health care can never be 'assured'. There is no gold standard according to which quality can be assessed or even consensus among experts about what constitutes good quality and how it might be measured. The task facing hospitals is to design a coherent framework in which information relevant to quality can be handled and assessments made of what information is of use.

That is not to say that patient evaluations of care should not be valued or that complaints systems cannot be of use to quality assurance programmes. There are other and much better ways of obtaining patient ratings through patient satisfaction surveys and many of the problems discussed above can be mitigated by reference to them. At its most productive the complaints system's use for a hospitals quality programme will probably be incidental to other goals, which, it could be argued, are much more important. A system which genuinely operates to achieve the goals of investigation, provision of redress, explanation and satisfaction to the complainant can have pay-offs for quality assurance purposes. Changing the system to promote these goals would incidentally increase managerial and clinical accountability and foster better channels and flow of information.

NOTES

1 A review of the quality assurance literature illustrates that the term itself does not have an accepted definition and that its meaning is the subject of fierce debate. In the present context it is sufficient to say that it most commonly involves the design of quality standards; the assessment of whether or not these are being met; and the modification of such standards where appropriate. The process can be applied to all aspects of hospital care. Nick Black (1990) has argued that, although observers might be forgiven for believing that quality assurance was invented in the 1980s, much of the philosophy and methodology of quality assurance had been established before that time.

2 The pressure to adopt quality assurance programmes must be seen against the backdrop of the rise in consumerism, a political consensus that many large UK public sector concerns such as the NHS had grown remote and the increase in cost containment measures. One of the main arguments of *Working for Patients* was that reorganization and increased accountability, rather than the investment of more money, are the answers to the problems faced in the NHS.

3 The broad aims of that research are to provide information about the sources of user grievances and the distribution, treatment and outcome of complaints. The project is examining the system from the complainant and organizational perspectives and is also considering the efficiency and effectiveness of current procedures. The research is funded by the Economic and Social Research Council.

4 Although the guidance governing the operation of the hospital complaints procedure assumes that most complaints will be made by patients, a substantial proportion received by health authorities are not. In one of the districts in our study 125 out of 185 complaints registered in a two-year period were made by non-patient complainants. The complainants were most commonly mothers (21 per cent); daughters (19 per cent) or husbands (14 per cent) of the patient whom the complaint related to. In some of the 125 cases the complaint related solely to something experienced by the non-patient complainant.

5 The two groups of complainants are collectively referred to as health service 'users' in this chapter.

6 A unit usually consists of an acute hospital or group of services linked together in some way, e.g. mental health or community.

7 The procedure itself was introduced in England from 1 September 1981, in Wales from 1 December 1981 and in Scotland from 1 January 1982.

8 One of the things argued in *Working for Patients* is that there is a need for clearer and more sensitive procedures for making suggestions on how the system might be improved. With this in mind, booklets have been circulated to every household in the country which contain, among other things, information on how to complain.

9 The Committee was appointed: to provide the hospital service with practical guidance in the form of a code of principles and practice for recording and investigating matters affecting patients which go wrong in hospitals; for receiving complaints or suggestions by patients, staff or others about such matters; and for communicating the results of investigations and to make recommendations.

10 Similar consumer awareness problems have been reported in other fields. See, for instance, Alan Andreasen (1975).

11 See, for instance, Gostin (1982). HC(81)5 did contain the suggestion that the general principles relating to hospital complaints should be applied to services provided by authorities outside hospitals. However, the circular was cancelled by HC(88)37 and the suggestion has not been officially revived.

12 See, for instance, the arguments of the National Consumer Council which suggest that the designated officer should be able to receive both types of complaint, initiate informal discussions between the complainant and any staff involved and, where appropriate, trigger examination of clinical complaints by the Regional Medical Officer and independent professional review. As long ago as 1973 the Davies Committee recommended that investigation of complaints should be the task of managers of the service (Department of Health and Social Security, 1973).

13 Letters of complaint very enormously not only in their content but in their method of presentation. The complaint may be expressed in one sentence or in a lengthy account running to several pages.

14 See Table 5, *Report on the Operation of Procedure for Independent Review of Complaints involving the Clinical Judgement of Hospital Doctors and Dentists*, 1983.

15 These were in response to complaints about inadequate care of road accident victims, inadequate antenatal monitoring and delay in delivery following diagnosis of intrauterine death, and failure in diagnosis and inappropriate discharge respectively.

16 An interesting literature is developing in the States which suggests, contrary to the popular stereotype, that Americans are not litigious, that they prefer avoidance or negotiation to other modes of dispute resolution. See, for example, Greenhouse (1986).

17 For the most recent example see the Harvard Study (1990).

18 One of the aims of our study is to assess the impact that prior contact with the hospital complained about has on propensity to complain.

4   Recent developments in medical quality assurance and audit
An international comparative study

Timothy Stoltzfus Jost

This chapter grew out of the hope, which inspires comparative research, that there might be lessons to be learned from the experience of others. The author, an American, was interested in the problem of how government might go about assuring the quality of medical care, a topic of great current importance in the United States. The Medicare Peer Review (PRO) Programme of quality regulation costs $255 million a year and a recent report from the Institute of Medicine has called for this to be further strengthened (Institute of Medicine 1990). There have been frequent calls for state professional disciplinary efforts to be strengthened which have led to the creation of a new federal databank to which all malpractice settlements and judgements and hospital and professional disciplinary actions must be reported. The volume of medical malpractice suits based on allegations of poor quality medical care is notorious and involving ever higher sums of money. It is not clear, however, that all this activity and expense is significantly improving the quality of American medical care.

This study started from the assumption that European states, which have been financing medical care through public or quasi-public means for decades, would have developed efficient and effective means of assuring the quality of medical care, from which the United States could learn. They would, surely, have had an interest in making certain that they were purchasing high quality medical care and have developed mechanisms for monitoring and policing standards.

As the study progressed, however, it became clear that Europe has not taken up the particular model of external quality review adopted in the US and its experience was not directly relevant to American concerns. What was striking, however, was the amount which Europeans could, potentially, learn from each other. There is a great deal of activity using other approaches to medical quality assurance but the various European states seem to be proceeding in similar directions with little recognition of the common ground between them.

Target 31 of the 'Strategy for Health for All by the Year 2000' of the Regional Committee for Europe of the World Health Organization – the nearest approximation to an official pan-European health policy statement – reads: 'By 1990, all Member States should have built effective mechanisms for ensuring the quality of patient care within their health care systems' (WHO 1985: 116). Though no country has yet achieved this goal, West Germany[1] adopted legislation mandating quality assurance efforts in both the ambulatory and institutional sectors from 1 January 1989 (SGB V, ss. 135–137); Belgium enacted a hospital law, which came into effect on 6 May 1988, requiring 'appropriate measures for the improvement and permanent evaluation of the quality of medicine in hospital' (AR, 7 August 1987, article 124); and medical audit is a key part of Britain's recent White Paper, *Working for Patients*, on the reorganization of the National Health Service (Department of Health 1989a; 1989b).

These quality assurance strategies are quite different from those currently being pursued in the United States. They depend on professionals reviewing each other's work rather than on scrutiny directed by government or insurers; they are based on educational rather than punitive interventions; and they are often focused on particular conditions or problems rather than on the performance of individuals. Nevertheless, comparison between the American and European approaches will not be abandoned completely. Ultimately, we must ask whether Europe's current path will prove satisfactory: will Europe be able to avoid the external intervention that is increasingly common in the United States? We must also consider whether the United States should learn from Europe: did we abandon too quickly the path Europe is still travelling (Berwick 1989)?

METHODOLOGY AND SCOPE

This chapter is concerned with efforts to assure quality in medical care. More specifically, it is focused on quality assurance efforts affecting care provided by doctors and hospitals. This is not to slight important developments in quality assurance affecting other health care professionals or the supply of products, such as pharmaceuticals, but rather to concentrate on the medical care providers who consume the most resources and probably have the greatest effect on patients, for good or ill.

'Quality assurance' here refers to programmes that set standards, assess the performance of professionals or institutions with respect to these standards, encourage improvement where performance can be improved, and attempt corrective action where the non-compliance is unacceptable. Standards may be explicit or implicit, corrective actions may be informational, educational or punitive. 'Medical audit' is defined more narrowly to include programmes in which doctors review each others' work for educational or informational purposes.

To discuss quality assurance, one must define what is meant by quality. European commentators tend to use a broad definition which covers scientific/technical knowledge and skills, effectiveness, adequacy, efficiency, acceptability to patients, and, under some definitions, also accessibility and equity (Blanpain 1985; Maxwell 1984; Shaw 1986a; Towell 1987; Vouri 1982). The term can, in fact, be defined so broadly as to include almost everything that might be considered desirable in health care. This study used a somewhat narrower definition, common in the United States, which focuses on the technical appropriateness and efficacy and the relational and communicational acceptability of care. It is less directly concerned with equity or economy.

The study examined recent quality assurance initiatives in four European countries: Sweden, the Federal Republic of Germany, Belgium and England.[2] These four were chosen to represent a range of approaches to the organization of health care. To simplify grossly, in Sweden and England health care is both provided and paid for by the state; in Belgium and West Germany health care is privately provided (though many hospitals are publicly owned) and financed through mandatory quasi-public insurance.

The report is part of a larger study, published by the King's Fund (Jost 1990), which was based on interviews with nearly eighty experts on the relevant health care systems and on an extensive review of English language literature and a more selective review of German and French language literature on medical care quality assurance in the subject countries. The larger study also considered more traditional regulatory approaches to quality assurance, including medical education, licensure and discipline, patient complaints programmes, insurance review, institutional inspection and medical negligence litigation.

England

Recent quality assurance and medical audit efforts in England have been the result of two concurrent, though sometimes conflicting, forces. First, the obsession of the Conservative government with efficiency, consumer service, strong business-like management and accountability in the NHS has led it to mandate programmes directed towards assuring that patients get value for their money (Department of Health and Social Security 1983; Department of Health 1989a). Second, the Royal Colleges (particularly the Royal College of General Practitioners, and more recently the Royal Colleges of Physicians and of Surgeons), the King's Fund and a number of academic institutions have, as a product of their mission to improve the practice of medicine, initiated a variety of quality assurance and medical audit programmes (Devlin 1988; Pollitt 1987; Royal College of General Practitioners 1985a; 1985b; Royal College of Physicians 1990; Royal College of Surgeons 1989; Shaw 1986a).[3] These interests have produced a large number of diverse projects and programmes that fall loosely into the categories of quality assurance and medical audit.

The 1983 NHS Management Inquiry by Sir Roy Griffiths, which generally proposed a more business-like approach to management in the NHS, found that Regions and Districts were not paying enough attention to the quality of the product provided to consumers (Department of Health and Social Security 1983). In response, the Department required each Region and District to designate a quality assurance officer. This task was usually assigned to Directors of Nursing or District Nursing Officers as an extension of their existing duties.

The origin of NHS quality assurance programmes in management concern for consumer satisfaction and their direction by nurses has largely determined their content. Programmes commonly address the 'shop window' concerns of management or the care delivery concerns of nurses (Adam 1987; National Audit Office 1988; Shaw 1988). Issues often covered include waiting times for operations, waiting times for out-patient clinics, cleanliness, patient comfort, palatability of food, patient dignity and privacy and communication with patients (O'Brien 1987). It has been less common for doctors to be involved in quality assurance programmes, which have, therefore, seldom addressed the technical provision of medical care (Shaw 1987). These programmes received little direction from the Department of Health or from the NHS Management Board and varying support from Regional and District management. There was widespread 'confusion and lack of clarity' among District General Managers as to what quality assurance was supposed to achieve (Templeton College 1987: 13). The programmes often had to proceed with minimal resources, particularly in Districts where they lacked management backing. As a result, they have tended to be grass roots efforts, with much duplication and uneven effectiveness. A recent NHS management directive has provided some guidance. It requires all Districts to introduce quality assurance systems, focusing, predictably, on appointment systems, informational leaflets for patients, the appearance of public and reception areas, and the use of customer satisfaction surveys (NHS Management Executive 1989).

Despite the obstacles, quality assurance programmes have continued to grow in number and sophistication. They have received valuable support from academic and health research centres.[4] Their directors have formed a National Association of Quality Assurance which is co-ordinating their efforts through conferences, publications and other networking efforts (see

National Association of Quality Assurance 1988). They are beginning to set standards for services and to use these as a basis for evaluation. Consumer satisfactions and dissatisfactions are being monitored through surveys and complaint review. This wide variety of educational and research activities is undoubtedly having a positive effect on the quality of patient care.

Medical audit programmes, by contrast, focus on care delivered by physicians. The most venerable medical audit programme in England is the Confidential Enquiry into Maternal Deaths in England and Wales, which has monitored maternal mortality and published triennial reports since 1952. Most maternal deaths during this period have been reviewed by the District medical officer, under whatever title he has been known, whose report is reviewed by the Regional obstetrics assessor and the Department of Health's central obstetrics assessors. The programme's triennial report analyses the causes of avoidable deaths. During the thirty-three years covered by the eleven published reports, the maternal mortality rate in England and Wales fell from 989 per million maternities in 1951 to 86 in 1984 (Department of Health 1989c). The Confidential Enquiry into Perioperative Deaths sponsored by the King's Fund and Nuffield Provincial Hospital Trust and carried out by the Associations of Surgeons and Anaesthetists of Great Britain and Ireland in 1985 and 1986 has undertaken a similar review of deaths caused by surgery (Buck *et al.* 1988; Devlin 1988). This project has now become a national effort in which virtually all surgeons in the United Kingdom are participating (National Confidential Enquiry into Perioperative Deaths 1989). It has expanded its scope to compare the treatment of patients who die in surgery with that of similar patients who survive, and to review randomly the treatment of at least one patient per year of every participating surgeon.

Medical audit has also been supported by the Royal Colleges (Shaw 1986b). The Royal College of General Practitioners has strongly supported medical audit among GPs (Pendleton *et al.* 1986; Royal College of General Practitioners 1985b), and has devised a tool for assessing what it identifies as the four most important qualities of GPs: professional values, accessibility, clinical competence and ability to communicate (Royal College of General Practitioners 1985a). The College both audits and requires audit within practices engaged in GP training. It has also recently initiated a Practice Activity Analysis Programme, in which doctors discuss with each other variations in their practice patterns in an attempt to become more aware of what they do and why (Crombie and Fleming 1988).

The Royal College of Physicians of London has recently produced a programme for medical audit and has sponsored several outcome studies on a regional or district level (Royal College of Physicians 1989). The Royal College of Surgeons has also published an audit programme, which it will use to review training placements (Royal College of Surgeons 1989). Other audit programmes are being carried out on a smaller scale by physicians in individual hospitals or districts (Ham and Hunter 1988; Royal College of Physicians 1989).

The government has recently seized the initiative on medical audit. *Working for Patients*, the 1989 Health Service White Paper, envisaged the establishment of medical audit in both the hospital and primary care sector by 1991 (Department of Health 1989a; 1989b). The White Paper defined medical audit as 'a systematic, critical analysis of the quality of medical care, including the procedures used for diagnosis and treatment, the use of resources, and the resulting outcome for the patient' (Department of Health 1989a: 39). It is to be based on confidential physician peer review and directed by a District medical audit advisory committee in the hospital sector and by an FPC medical audit advisory committee in the primary care sector.[5] Participation will be universal and compulsory, not voluntary, as has always previously been the case. While medical audit will be medically led, it will also be accountable to management, which will receive a report on the general results and may initiate its own independent audit where it is dissatisfied with a particular service. Initially responses to poor quality would be corrective and educational in nature, but in the long run management may be given more direct means of intervention.

The profession's response to these proposals has ranged from cautious support to deep suspicion (British Medical Association 1989; 'Called to Account' 1989). The tone of the rest of the White Paper, which stresses increased competition and management control over medical care, and its place in a long history of government reluctance to commit additional resources to the NHS, worry even those who generally support medical audit. They are concerned that the compulsory audit may bring additional work without additional resources and fear management interference with clinical freedom and breaches of patient confidentiality. Several experts interviewed for this study expressed misgivings that the government's support of medical audit would discourage rather than encourage support for the concept among doctors.

The debate over medical audit provoked by the White Paper highlights some of the difficulties with establishing quality assurance programmes in the UK. First, the British government, which spends less on health care than any of the other countries studied, may be reluctant to meet the costs that could result from serious quality assurance efforts (see Griggs 1989). Quality assurance and medical audit can save money, but they can also identify the need for additional resources. Some suspect that the reluctance of the government to support hospital accreditation, an idea championed by the King's Fund (Brooks 1989), may be partly based on its unwillingness to commit the resources necessary to bring facilities up to accreditation standards. Second, the principle of clinical autonomy is held particularly dear by British physicians (Harrison and Schulz 1989; Hoffenberg 1986; Miller 1987). Medical audit necessarily lays a doctor open to scrutiny by others and will face opposition from many physicians for that reason alone. If audit is to be accountable to management, the scale of opposition is likely to be even greater. Finally, the information systems necessary for comprehensive medical audit and quality assurance are still largely undeveloped in the UK. In particular, the performance indicators which are readily available are criticized for providing little assistance in evaluating health care (Harley 1988; Jenkins *et al.* 1987). Appropriate information can only be produced with an additional commitment of resources, which may not be forthcoming. The monitoring systems will also have to deal with concerns about patient confidentiality.

There is much enthusiasm for quality assurance and medical audit in the UK, which has led to some impressive accomplishments. But their impact is still very uneven and there are substantial barriers to comprehensive and universal programmes.

The Federal Republic of Germany

The current state of health care quality assurance in the Federal Republic bears some rather striking resemblances to developments in England.[6] In Germany, as in England, two traditions of quality assurance have developed, one sponsored by professional associations and oriented towards the collection and analysis of outcome data, the other sponsored primarily by those who pay for the care – in Germany, the *Kassenärztliche Vereinigungen* (organizations of insurance doctors, here KVs) rather than the government – and designed not to interfere with the clinical practice of medicine. However, the 1988 German Health Reform Act, like the White Paper in England, indicates a heightening of government interest in physician accountability.

Quality assurance in Germany has, though, a uniquely German flavour. This is most clearly evident in the legal structure for quality assurance created by the 1988 Act. The programme will not be supervised by the government but by the co-operative efforts of the self-governing organizations of medical providers and insurers. There is also a distinctive emphasis on technological accuracy rather than the broader concerns of the English.

For over a decade the Federal KV (sometimes together with the insurance funds) has issued quality guidelines defining physician qualifications and technical equipment requirements for the ambulatory sector, which it oversees (see Flatten 1988; Sachverständigenrat 1989; Schwartz 1984). If providers are to be reimbursed by the social insurance system, they must comply with these guidelines. In several areas these guidelines form the basis for quality assurance review programmes. A few of these are also extended to the institutional sector through joint programmes with the federal *Ärztekammer* (physician chamber, here AK) or by federal law.

Since 1977 the KV has required members who use their own laboratories for clinical chemistry to participate in 'ring trials', which use external controls to assure the comparability of laboratory results (Beske 1989; Selbmann 1982). More recently the KV has begun to require controls through specimens, phantoms or peer review of pictures for radiology, ultrasound and nuclear imaging. Under recent amendments to the Weights and Measures Act, these measures also apply to the institutional sector. Quality assurance in radiology is required by recent federal regulations (Bundesärztekammer 1989, Sachverständigenrat 1989). Radiology quality assurance will be supervised by a programme jointly sponsored by the federal KV and AK. The *Bundesausschusse*, the federal committee of the KV and insurance funds, has also issued guidelines for cancer and children's screening, antenatal care and psychotherapy. The psychotherapy guidelines require second opinions in particular cases (Sachverständigenrat 1989). Further guidelines concerning professional and technical qualifications have been issued by the federal or by Land KVs for other areas including nuclear medicine, long-term electrocardiograms, cytology and microbiology (Sachverständigenrat 1989). Finally, the scientific committees of the federal AK have issued a number of recommendations about the provision of care in various specialties, although, unlike the guidelines of the KV, it is not possible to enforce compliance with these by denying reimbursement to delinquent providers (Sachverständigenrat 1989).

The other great tradition in German quality assurance programmes is that of professionally sponsored outcome studies. The oldest of these is the series of studies in perinatology sponsored by the AK and KV, which began in Munich in 1975. The programme now covers the entire country, including 820 hospitals with about 490,000 births per year (Beske *et al.* 1988; Beske 1989). Data are collected on the risks and complications of pregnancy and births, and reported to participating hospitals in the form of biennial, hospital-specific and problem-related statistics. Between 1974 and 1986 the rate of perinatal mortality in Bavaria dropped from 26.3 per thousand to 7.1 per thousand (Beske *et al.* 1988). In 1980 and 1984 similar voluntary post-operative studies were carried out in gynaecology, documenting, for participating hospitals, the comparative frequency of complications, pre-operative risk factors and post-operative morbidity (Beske *et al.* 1988). Studies evaluating the quality of surgical interventions have been carried out in the states of North Rhein-Westphalia and Baden-Wurtemberg (Besk *et al.* 1988; Schega 1984). These studies focus on tracer diagnoses (most commonly, cholelithiasis, inguinal hernia and fracture of the femur) and again provide participating hospitals with comparative process and outcome information. Pilot studies are also being carried out in vascular surgery, neurosurgery, heart surgery and paediatrics (Beske *et al.* 1988; Sachverständigenrat 1989).

These studies share a number of characteristics. Most are sponsored by professional organizations, such as the AKs, KVs or German Surgical Society and are facilitated by academic institutions. Participation by physicians and hospitals is voluntary. Information is collected on a broad basis through relatively simple questionnaires. The identity of patients and doctors is kept confidential. Information on particular hospitals is revealed only to the chief physicians of the relevant hospital department; third parties receive anonymous data. Department chiefs may use the information as they see fit.

The 1988 German Health Reform Law makes quality assurance mandatory in both the primary and institutional care sectors. Section 135 (SGB V) prohibits payment for new diagnostic and treatment methods under social insurance until such methods have been recognized by the federal committee of the KVs and insurance funds, and these bodies have established professional and technical qualifications and process guidelines for their use. This section gives legal backing to guidelines which the KVs previously issued voluntarily.

Section 136 (SGB V) goes further, requiring the KVs to examine the quality of care provided in particular cases by sampling insured people receiving ambulatory care and reviewing the choice, extent and process of treatment. The federal committee of the insurance funds and the KVs is to establish guidelines for this quality review.

Section 137 (SGB V) requires hospitals receiving social insurance payments to carry out quality assurance measures. These must deal with treatment, the course of medical care, including the use of second opinions before surgery, and outcomes. The results will have to be reported in a way which will allow comparisons to be made between hospitals. Guidelines for this exercise will be established at the state level by the associations representing the insurance funds and the hospital owners. Finally, sections 138 and 139 (SGB V) require the KVs and insurance funds to ensure the quality and effectiveness of new medical remedies and devices.

The 1988 law, however, was built on previous developments, which have shaped its implementation. Since 1986 the federal medical association and hospital association had had a co-operation agreement to facilitate quality assurance measures. Several co-operative programmes were under way at the Land level, including programmes in North Rhein, Baden-Württemberg and Schleswig-Holstein (Beske *et al.* 1989; Sachverständigenrat 1989). The draft agreement among the insurance companies, the German hospital association, and German medical associations on the implementation of the 1988 law build on these precedents. In accordance with recommendations from the 1989 report of the Concerted Action group which makes recommendations for health policy in Germany, they envisage the extension of the pre-existing perinatal, neonatal and surgical quality assurance programmes to all hospitals. The drafts also contemplate further measures dealing with duration of stay, medical records, use of drugs (especially antibiotics and blood products), use of laboratory and radiology services, use of invasive or costly diagnostic and therapeutic procedures, operative wound infections and unexpected results (mortality, complications, re-admissions) (Sachverständigenrat 1989). They call for improved data reporting by hospitals, based on reporting requirements established in 1986 for diagnostic data. The drafts contemplate the creation of a board of trustees representing the participants in the agreement to review the reports of specialists interpreting hospital data, but hold firmly to the principle that data identifying patients, doctors or hospitals should not be disclosed to third parties.

It is less clear how quality assurance review will be carried out in the ambulatory sector. Comments on the government's initial draft suggested that the quality examination might be combined with the insurance efficiency review system described above (Bundesrat 1988). Experts interviewed speculated that review might be focused on doctors who are the subject of complaints rather than carried out at random.

The new law requires the KVs and insurance funds to develop guidelines governing professional practice. This has traditionally been the domain of the physician chambers and, as might be expected, the federal physician chamber has strongly objected to this development (Bundesärztekammer 1989). In general, though, the provisions of the 1988 law seem to have provoked relatively little controversy, despite going further than the laws of any of the other countries studied. One expert interviewed, who had followed the developments of the 1988 Health Reform Law closely for two years, was unaware of these provisions. It is not difficult to see why this is so. The law respects the self-governing structure of German health care and makes no radical changes undermining professional power. Quality assurance programmes are to be directed by the medical, hospital and insurance associations without interference from the government.[7] The confidentiality of review results will continue to be preserved. Quality improvement will be achieved through education rather than sanctions. Implementation will proceed slowly, beginning with the development of guidelines at federal level, followed by the elaboration of details at Land and provider level. Everyone interviewed expected that several years would pass before the law was fully implemented. Quality assurance will remain a function internal to the medical professions, beyond external review.

Belgium

It is difficult to assess the current state of medical quality assurance efforts in Belgium.[8] Belgium was the first of the four countries studied to adopt, on 7 August 1987, a comprehensive legal requirement for hospital-based quality assurance. However, several experts interviewed thought that little had happened to implement this law, and that the real achievements of quality assurance in Belgium had been at the level of individual hospitals.

As in England and West Germany, the professional associations and the organizations paying for care (here the mutual insurance funds through the *Institut Nationale d'Assurance Maaldie-Invalidité* or INAMI) can point to some achievements in the area of quality assurance. One is the indirect effects of the insurance funds' economic review programmes, which focus primarily on detecting inefficiency and fraud but also consider quality issues. Another is the long-standing requirement that the quality of the work done by biological laboratories must be externally reviewed before the laboratories can collect reimbursement from insurers.

The perinatal monitoring projects of the *Vlaamse Vereniging voor Obstetrie en Gynecologie* (Flemish Society for Obstetrics and Gynaecology) and the *Groupement des Gynécologues de Langue Française de Belgique* (Grouping of French-Speaking Gynaecologists of Belgium) are important examples of the quality assurance efforts of professional organizations (Buekens *et al.* 1987; Derom *et al.* 1989). These studies involve the confidential collection of data from maternity units, with feedback reports allowing the units to compare outcomes among themselves. As in Germany and England, participation is voluntary and unit-specific data are not made available to third parties. The Flemish report form includes sixty-five items, and focuses on test data, such as blood pressure or urinary protein levels, rather than on diagnostic data, to avoid diagnostic inaccuracies or differences of interpretation (Derom *et al.* 1989). The French sector has a similar approach but uses different data collection procedures since the French hospitals are more fully computerized and the project needs only to collate existing data.

In Belgium (again as in England and West Germany) the focus of quality assurance efforts has changed from voluntary initiatives to externally mandated programmes. Belgium has, for some time, had standards, enforced by a system of inspection, governing the physical plant, organization and staffing of hospitals. In 1987, however, as part of a law restructuring the organization of its hospitals, Belgium laid down statutory responsibilities for quality assurance within each hospital. Since 6 May 1988, the head doctor of each hospital has been responsible for ensuring that there are 'organizational structures allowing for a systematic process of evaluation of medical practice' in his or her hospital (AR, 7 August 1987 arts. 15, 16). A royal decree of 15 December 1987 further specified that the head doctor was responsible for keeping records of medical activities and the organization of medical auditing (s. 6). Each hospital's Medical Council, which represents its doctors, must also ensure that they collaborate on suitable measures for:

1 encouraging, and permanently evaluating, the quality of medicine practised at the hospital;
2 promoting a team spirit among the hospital doctors;
3 encouraging collaboration with other members of the hospital personnel and, in particular, with the nursing and paramedical staff;
4 promoting collaboration between the hospital's doctors and other doctors, in particular the general practitioner or the consultant who referred the patient;
5 stimulating medical activity of a scientific nature, having regard to the resources of the hospital.

(AR, 7 August 1987, s. 124)

Department heads must co-operate with the head doctor in carrying out quality assurance activities (AR, 15 December 1987, art. 19). Finally, all medical staff are responsible for collaborating in the evaluation of care, including the discussion of policies for admissions and discharges, prescription and distribution of medicines, and medical audit (AR, 15 December 1985, art. 20).

The law leaves most decisions about how to pursue quality evaluation to individual hospitals. In a few respects, however, it is more prescriptive. There are detailed requirements about the composition of hospital patient records and summaries of these must be kept in such a way as to permit the permanent evaluation of medical work. A royal decree of 7 November 1988 requires hospitals to set up hygiene committees responsible for infection control.

Moreover, the Community Council of Health Care Establishments of the French sector (CCES) has proposed additional requirements such as internal evaluation of personal treatment of patients, staff members and nursing care, ethics committees, medical audit and interdisciplinary evaluation of care (Anrys 1988). The CCES proposes to create a Central Committee for the Evaluation of the Quality of Care (CEQUAS), which would carry out external audits of hospitals through inspections. CEQUAS inspectors would give technical assistance to the hospitals, but also inform the CCES about the quality of care in each establishment (Anrys 1988; Roger 1988).

The infrastructure is developing within Belgium to give effect to such requirements. For some years minimum clinical information on hospital patients has been collected centrally and nursing information is now being added to this. These data could be used for external assessment of hospital quality assurance efforts. According to one source, the Ministry of Health has begun to hire inspectors to evaluate hospitals' quality assurance programmes. The Belgian Federation of Doctors has created an advisory group to assist hospitals in establishing quality assurance programmes and to serve as a clearing house for information.

Nevertheless, most of the experts interviewed thought that the real situation in most Belgian hospitals had not kept pace with the legal developments. In part his reflects the inevitable time lag between the adoption of laws and compliance with them. But other forces are also at work. First, and most important, the new requirements have not been accompanied by new funding.[9] In Belgium, where hospital reimbursement is calculated through a complex formula which only takes account of enumerated cost items, there is understandable resistance to taking on additional responsibilities which are not matched by additional resources. Moreover, the vagueness of the law has left a good deal of uncertainty as to what compliance requires. Some hospitals, for example, believe that hospital-based scientific research activities are sufficient to comply with the law, whether or not they result in changes in patient care.

There are notable quality assurance programmes at individual hospitals. The nursing quality education and promotion programme of A. Jacquerye at Érasme Hospital in Brussels is one example (Jacquerye 1987). Another is the quality assurance of J.-P. Gassee at Brugmann Hospital, also in Brussels, which has carried out evaluation studies of the use of digoxin, treatment of hand fractures, blood transfusions and theophylline dosage monitoring. It remains to be seen, however, if and when the practice of quality assurance in hospitals, required by law, will become universal.[10]

Sweden

Sweden has pursued a very different course from the other countries covered by this study.[11] As far as could be determined, there has been no national data collection by professional associations to compare with the studies on perinatal, maternal or surgical mortality and morbidity found elsewhere. There is a national system for the reporting of medical accidents and data are collected centrally on drug side-effects and X-ray use. Otherwise Sweden has no national regulatory programme or legislation promoting quality assurance or medical audit.

Sweden has not, however, been inactive over quality assurance. Rather, the government's approach has been to facilitate rather than to mandate quality assurance, trusting the health care system to respond to information if this is provided. The primary agency in this effort is SPRI, the Swedish Planning and Rationalization Institute for Health and Social Services, which is jointly owned by the Swedish government and the Federation of County Councils (SPRI 1986). A number of other national agencies, including the National Board of Health and Welfare, the Swedish Medical Research Council and the Swedish Council on Technology Assessment in Health Care, also contribute towards improving the quality of Swedish health care.

The most significant Swedish initiative for quality assurance (as broadly defined) is technology assessment. Over the past decade, SPRI has been involved in a variety of programmes evaluating and setting standards for the use of medical technologies. Its health economics section has produced a number of reports on subjects such as computerized tomography, ultrasound diagnostics, magnetic resonance imaging, care of the elderly, and variations in the use of technology in obstetrics and gynaecology. SPRI and the Swedish Medical Research Council have held several joint consensus conferences evaluating technologies such as the artificial hip, care of myocardial infarction, and diagnosis and treatment of cerebral haemorrhage and stroke. During 1988, its first year of operation, the Swedish Council on Technology Assessment in Health Care undertook nine studies including a review of pre-operative routines, assessment of treatment methods for back pain, and assessment of the value of vascular surgery for vascular spasms in the legs.

While these programmes are not traditional quality assurance or medical audit programmes, they contribute to those goals. They are not narrow technical evaluations but deal broadly with the efficacy, efficiency and humanitarian and social acceptability of medical procedures. In so far as they facilitate the introduction and development of guidelines for the use of effective technologies and deter the introduction, or assist in the elimination, of invalid technologies, they make an important contribution to the quality of health care.[12] They may also set standards for quality assessment programmes, if these are set up in the future.

The Swedish initiative which has attracted most international attention has been SPRI's Medical Care Programmes Project (Eckerlund 1986; Pine *et al.* 1988; Vouri 1989). Medical Care Programmes develop comprehensive standards, adapted to local resources, for the prevention, diagnosis, treatment and follow-up of various health care conditions. They tend to focus on conditions that require primary care over a period of time, unlike other technology assessment programmes that concentrate on particular procedures or on equipment. Though these programmes have been acclaimed by some, they have also been criticized as being too complex and too standardized to be of use in the everyday treatment of disease and for taking too much effort to develop.

Another SPRI initiative has been its patient satisfaction survey project (SPRI 1987). Patient satisfaction surveys developed by SPRI are currently being used in sixty-eight of Sweden's eighty acute care hospitals. Some of these hospitals compare their results with a large data bank compiled by SPRI. It is interesting that England, the only other country in this study with publicly provided health care, is the only other country that has used patient satisfaction surveys extensively. These instruments may compensate to some degree for the absence of a market for health care provision in the two countries.

Most quality assurance efforts in Sweden, however, take place at the local level, often facilitated by SPRI. The informal Stockholm Health Care Evaluation Group, for example, sponsors a variety of quality assurance programmes within Stockholm County (Reizenstein *et al.* 1987). These projects include the study of variations in femoral neck fracture surgery, X-ray use and record management. Patient satisfaction with hospital meals is being monitored, as is compliance with medical care programmes for four different diseases. Targeted medical audits and studies of bed occupancy rates are planned or in progress. SPRI has initiated quality circle programmes in other counties and is currently designing a project to install comprehensive quality assurance programmes in three hospitals.

It is difficult to evaluate the comparative effectiveness of Sweden's non-interventionist approach to quality assurance. It is certainly consistent with the Swedish emphasis on consensus building and educative approaches to problem-solving. It must also be seen in the context of Sweden's system of complaint investigation and medical discipline, which provides more extensive external supervision of medical care than is found in any of the other countries studied. Nevertheless, several of the experts interviewed seemed to believe that Sweden was lagging behind in the area of quality assurance, that little was happening in many hospitals and that the quality of care was suffering because of this.

CONCLUDING OBSERVATIONS

An American reviewing the current state of quality assurance in these four European countries cannot but be struck by the extent to which they rely on the medical profession to ensure the quality of its members' performance. This is in stark contrast to the United States, which relies increasingly on external controls to ensure the quality of medical care. This process is most obvious in medical malpractice litigation, where American judges and lay juries assess the performance of the doctors brought before them. There are also the Medicare Peer Review Organizations, which, though run by doctors, are directly accountable to the government for their performance; state physician licensure boards, which increasingly include consumer members and are seen as agencies of state governments rather than as representatives of medical associations; and state and local health departments inspecting institutions such as nursing homes and hospitals. Moreover, quality regulation in the United States increasingly relies on sanctions, such as malpractice judgements, the withdrawal or suspension of licences to practice, exclusion from federal health insurance programmes (Medicare and Medicaid) or fines to police physician performance.

The countries studied here still place considerable trust in the medical profession to police itself. This policing is accomplished through educational rather than punitive interventions, and there is little apparent interest in following the United States towards external control (Pollitt 1987). Legislation in West Germany and Belgium and proposed measures in England are directed towards encouraging more general peer review rather than expanding external oversight. The general goal seems to be to improve the performance of the profession by bringing up the average rather than by cutting off the tail of poor performers. Professionals are thought more likely to respond to education than to 'fear of the Gendarme' (Jacquerye 1987: 5). Although there was much admiration among experts interviewed for American hospital peer review systems, few in the professions, academia or government had much interest in emulating the American malpractice or PRO systems.

There is much to be said for not blindly following the American approach. First, it is proving very costly. The PRO budget for 1989 was $255 million. The direct costs of medical malpractice litigation are in excess of $4 billion and its indirect costs may be much higher. Moreover, the benefits of external review in terms of better medical care are not immediately obvious. Infant mortality rates are higher in the United States than in any of the countries studied. Life expectancy at birth for men is lower in the United States than in any of the countries studied except Belgium. More directly related to medical care, the rate of death in the United States from infectious and parasitical diseases is twice that of Belgium, Sweden and West Germany and three times that of England. The rate of death from septicaemia in the United States is nearly twice that of Belgium, four times that of West Germany and six times that of England

(WHO 1988). While one can argue about how to interpret epidemiological data, it does not appear that American medical care is dramatically better than that in Europe.

None the less, an American observer may be left feeling uncomfortable with the European approach to medical care quality assurance for several reasons. First, it is not clear that professional self-regulation can adequately address the problems caused by medical care financing systems that create incentives to withhold medical care from patients and set up a conflict between the pecuniary interest of doctors and the medical needs of patients. It was the fear of such incentives created by the adoption of Diagnosis Related Group hospital prospective payment by Medicare that led to the creation of the quality oversight functions of Medicare Peer Review Organizations in the United States. In none of the countries studied are such forms of reimbursement yet widespread. Belgium and West Germany rely on fee for service payment of doctors; in Sweden and England most doctors are effectively salaried.[13] Several countries are considering prospective payment or capitation, however, and some experts thought that external review of quality could become necessary if such systems were implemented. Significantly, the British White Paper which proposed self-governing hospitals and GP budgets also envisaged management oversight of medical audit (see Griggs 1989).

Second, professional self-regulation has traditionally proved largely ineffective for removing incompetents from the medical professions, at least in instances where their incompetence did not take forms that publicly embarrassed the professions. Where a doctor could not or would not deliver medical care of adequate quality because of venality, stupidity, laziness, addiction or superannuation, colleagues have responded, if at all, through the denial of social or professional contacts rather than by withdrawing a licence to practise (Freidson 1970). Although there has been some progress in dealing with substance abuse among doctors in the countries studied, there has been little movement towards dealing with incompetents. The strong hierarchical organization of hospitals in some European countries (most notably in Germany, though also to a lesser extent in Sweden and Belgium) may limit the damage done by incompetents, but more needs to be done to identify them and address the problems they cause.

Third, and perhaps most important, there is value in the accountability created by external oversight systems irrespective of whether they actually have a salutary influence on the quality of medical care. Such systems can call doctors to be responsible to society for the resources they consume and for the harm they cause. There is clearly an emerging concern in Europe for some form of medical accountability. It is evident in the Medical Responsibility Board in Sweden, in management supervision of medical audit in the

White Paper in England, in national and French community inspection of medical audit in Belgium, and in the role which the sickness funds are to play in establishing guidelines for quality assurance in Germany. Whether these attempts to create accountability will be adequate remains to be seen.

European nations may ultimately find some aspects of the American external control approach to quality assurance worth emulating. But there are also lessons that the United States can learn from Europe. In particular, several countries have gone much further than the US in devising approaches to quality assurance in the ambulatory sector.

The most important message, however, is how much European nations have to learn from each other. National and regional data collections are progressing independently in several countries with little sharing of information and results. Several countries are moving towards medical audit, but with little collaboration. The World Health Organization's Regional Office for Europe has done much to facilitate interest in quality assurance, particularly by bringing together interested parties and sponsoring a number of studies. The *International Journal of Quality Assurance*, the *European Regional Newsletter on Quality Assurance* and the King's Fund Centre's *Quality Assurance Abstracts* also contribute to this process. The EC is laying the groundwork for the first Europe-wide data collection effort, in the field of ambulatory surgery.

But European countries could do much more to share information and ideas. Multinational data collection efforts reviewing maternal mortality or perinatal or surgical clinical outcomes might discover significant variations in outcome among different health care systems, which could ultimately be linked to differences in structure or process. Technology assessment might proceed more rapidly and effectively on a multi-national basis, whether dealing with new high-tech equipment or different approaches to clinical management of medical problems. It is also possible that radiology or laboratory quality review could be pursued more efficiently on a multi-national basis.

European nations could learn from each other's approaches to quality assurance regulation. The English and West German maternal, perinatal and surgical outcome data collection programmes could be models for other countries which want a better understanding of the current performance of medical practice in specific areas. The Swedish health care programmes and the guidelines developed by the German federal organization of insurance doctors for ambulatory care delivery represent models of standard-setting for clinical practice which other countries might want to study.

This chapter does not advocate a model system for regulating the quality of physician and hospital care. Nor does it pretend to instruct any particular country in detail as to how to change its systems for assuring medical care quality. Rather it has attempted to describe a variety of quality assurance regulatory programmes currently being pursued, with greater or lesser success, by four countries. Each has its strengths and limitations but a careful comparison may identify the opportunities which each presents to contribute to the goal of building 'effective mechanisms for ensuring the quality of patient care'.

This report was written during the winter and spring of 1989 while the author was visiting the Centre for Socio-Legal Studies, Wolfson College, University of Oxford, funded by a Fulbright Western European regional research grant. The author wishes to thank R. Dingwall, M. Döhler, H. Ector, L. Mulcahy, C. Oldertz, R. Schäfer and R. van den Oever for helpful comments on earlier drafts; A. Wörmer, D. Oderberg and K. Berglid for assistance with translation; members of the Socio-Legal Centre (especially R. Dingwall, P. Fenn, D. Hughes, A. McGuire and L. Mulcahy) for encouragement and assistance; the King's Fund Centre for the use of its marvellous library; and all the people who graciously educated me about the health care systems of their countries in our interviews.

TABLE OF STATUTES

Belgium

Arrete Royal [AR], 7 August 1987, arts. 15, 16, 124
Arrete Royal [AR], 15 December 1987, arts. 6, 19, 20
Arrete Royal [AR], 7 November 1988

Federal Republic of Germany

Sozialgesetzbuch [SGB] V ss. 94, 135, 136, 137, 138, 139

NOTES

1 The fieldwork on which this chapter is based was carried out prior to German reunification. The former Federal Republic's approach is likely to dominate the provision for the unified state, but the original terminology has been retained to remind the reader of its historical context.
2 This chapter focuses primarily on England rather than on the entire United Kingdom because health care delivery structures and quality assurance systems vary between the constituent countries of the UK. Where data are available only for the entire UK or for Great Britain or where one system applies throughout the UK, the chapter will make it clear that the UK or Britain is the basis of reference rather than England.

3 What follows is also based on discussions with T. Brooks and C. Shaw, King's Fund Centre, London; L. Davies and D. Harmon, Birmingham Health Services Research Unit; H. Devlin, CEPOD, London; D. Fleming, Royal College of General Practitioners, Birmingham; A. Gatherer, Oxfordshire District Health Authority, Oxford; Sir R. Hoffenberg, Royal College of Physicians of London; D. Hudson, National Association of Quality Assurance, Abergavenny; D. MacPherson, R. Oliver and G. Rivett, Department of Health, London; and V. Nathanson, British Medical Association, London.

4 These include Bath University's Centre for Analysis of Social Policy, Birmingham University's Health Management Centre, the Nuffield Centre for Health Service Studies and York University's Centre for Health Economics. The King's Fund Centre has a special quality assurance project, and publishes a bi-monthly abstract of publications relevant to quality assurance in health care.

5 The functions of Family Practitioner Committees have since been taken over by Family Health Services Authorities.

6 This section is based in part on conversations with F. Beske and J. Brecht, Institute for Health Systems Research, Kiel; H.-P. Brauer and F. Strobrawa, Bundesärztekammer, Cologne; G. Brenner, Central Institute of the Kassenärztliche Vereinigung, Cologne; S. Eichhorn, German Hospital Institute, Dusseldorf; H.-K. Selbmann, Institute for Medical Information, Tübingen; R. Sengler, Ministry of Work and Social Affairs, Bonn; and K. Überla, Institute for Medical Information, Biometry and Epidemiology, Munich.

7 The Minister of Work and Social Affairs can promulgate guidelines for quality assurance in primary care, however, if the Bundesauschluss fails to do so (SGB V. s. 94).

8 Among useful sources are Anrys (1988) and Roger (1988). This section is also based on interviews with J. Blanpain, University of Leuven; P. Buekens and A. Jacquerye, Erasme Hospital, Brussels; J. Gasse, Brugmann Hospital, Brussels; and F. Roger, Catholic University of Louvain, Brussels.

9 Additional funding has been made available for infection control procedures.

10 None of the experts with whom I spoke or the literature I reviewed mentioned quality assurance efforts in the primary care sector in Belgium. A recent draft of an inventory of quality assurance activities in Europe (Klazinga 1989) also fails to mention any programmes in this area.

11 This section is based on interviews with E. Borgenhammer and M. Brommels, Nordic School of Public Health, Gothenburg; L. Cedergren and C. Legerius, SPRI, Stockholm; G. Ljunggren and P. Reizenstein, Karolinska Institute, Stockholm; E. Jonsson, Swedish Council on Technology Assessment, Stockholm; and K. Roos, Swedish Ministry of Health, Stockholm.

12 A number of other European countries beyond those included in this study are also engaged in technology assessment, including Denmark, Norway, the Netherlands and France (Ministry of Health and Social Affairs 1986).

13 Since the completion of the fieldwork in England, the changes to GP contracts and the introduction of a class of GP fundholders, who manage a fixed budget for treatments as well as professional services, have altered the position somewhat. In terms of its economic incentives, the old capitation system had operated much like a salary; these developments move the incentives closer to those identified under Medicare.

5 Legislating for health

The changing nature of regulation in the NHS

David Hughes and Alistair McGuire

The history of the British National Health Service since 1948 has been a chronicle of a service in constant flux. In the face of long-standing problems of cost containment, resource allocation and service rationalization, successive governments have sought solutions through a variety of organizational reforms, including a major rejigging of the NHS structure in 1974. But, as in other Western health care systems, the difficulties have proved to be stubbornly intractable. The 1980s, far from marking a period of consolidation and equilibrium, have seen the pace of reform quickening as the interval between successive service reorganizations diminishes.

This chapter charts the significant shifts in regulatory philosophy that have occurred during the last decade, particularly in relation to the 1982 NHS reorganization, the policy initiatives that culminated in the 1983 Griffiths Report, and the more wide-ranging changes introduced by the National Health Service and Community Care Act 1990. The focus is on the mechanisms of organizational and professional control rather than regulation through legal processes in the courts. While there is some truth in the view that continual remedial work to the facade of the NHS 'shop' has had little impact on behaviour within (Maynard 1988: 160), the reform initiatives of the last ten years have become increasingly radical in character. The first cracks are appearing in the post-war consensus that emerged out of the uneasy compromises on which the NHS was founded. Arguably, the Griffiths reforms and the 1990 Act represent the first steps towards fundamental change in the regulatory machinery that has shaped health care in the intervening years.

In the sections that follow we describe how critical decisions, taken when the service was established, have created a particular framework of regulation that is only now being called into question, and chart the abrupt policy shifts of the 1980s – first as centralism was challenged and then resurrected, and later, when a new language of decentralization, markets and incentives came to the fore. We go on to set organizational change in the NHS against the background of the wider climate of public sector management reform in the 1980s, and show how the 'standard' reform package needed to be adapted to address long-standing tensions between the administrative and professional segments of the health service and the crucial issue of professional autonomy.

THE LEGACY OF 1948

Despite widespread political consensus on the need for a radical overhaul of health care, the 1948 NHS was not the product of social engineering or blue-sky planning. Social historians agree that it emerged through evolution rather than revolution (Eckstein 1958; Pater 1981; Webster 1988). The buildings, facilities and staff for the new service already existed in over fifteen hundred local authority and voluntary hospitals and the independent general practitioners and ancillary professions. To a large extent the tripartite organizational structure of the new service was dictated by the form of pre-war health care. The local authority and voluntary hospitals were brought together in an amalgamated hospital service under new regional hospital boards; other public health, maternity and domiciliary services remained with local health authorities based loosely on old local government units; finally, there was a system of executive councils to administer general medical and dental services outside hospitals, which in effect replaced the insurance committees set up under the 1911 National Insurance Act.

The NHS was established against the background of intense and acrimonious debate between the major interest groups involved. Inevitably, the decisions taken mirrored the mix of pragmatism and pugnaciousness needed to overcome opposition – whether in terms of compromise or innovative attempts to move beyond existing models. Three characteristics of the 1948 NHS were to have special significance in shaping the service through to the 1980s.

First, while established under the incoming Labour government of 1945, the NHS represented a rejection of both the collectivist route advocated by the Socialist Medical Association (involving an extended public health service) and the insurance-based model of publicly financed, privately produced health care adopted in most Western countries. What emerged was a nationalized rather than a socialized service (Saville 1983), which placed existing institutions under the direction of the Minister of Health, who was himself accountable to Parliament. Although the government made concessions in other areas such as the rules on private practice and the independence of the teaching hospitals, it was determined that state finance should mean state control. Thus substantial delegated powers, which have been further extended by subsequent legislation, were vested in the Minister by the 1946 Act:

> It shall be the duty of the Minister of Health to promote the establishment in England and Wales of a comprehensive health service designed to secure improvement in the physical and mental state of the people of England and Wales and the prevention, diagnosis and treatment of illness, and for that purpose to provide or secure the effective provision of services in accordance with the following provisions of this Act.
>
> (Section 1)

The effect was to place the NHS in a constitutional and legal position unique among contemporary British institutions (Jacob and Davies 1987: ss. 1–011). It is unlike the nationalized industries because they are run by boards; it is different from local government because NHS authority members are appointed rather than elected; and it differs from a government department because it is the health authority, rather than central government, that employs staff and determines significant aspects of administration.

Second, the decision to implement a nationalized system effectively foreclosed the option of a plurality of provider units. Interestingly, in view of the recent emergence of the concept of an 'internal market' within the NHS, the 1944 White Paper (Ministry of Health 1944) had proposed that contracts should be placed with the voluntary hospitals to secure the use of their facilities for the new service. Aneurin Bevan, Minister of Health in the 1945 Labour government, took the view that such pluralism would create difficulties within a comprehensive, state-financed system. 'How', he asked, 'can the State enter into a contract with a citizen to render service through an autonomous body?' (quoted by Watkin 1978: 18). Bevan contended that if the Minister was to be invested with statutory duties to provide health services, he must have full control over the means of doing so in the form of a unified hospital service.

Third, the foundation of the NHS rested on a pact between government and the doctors. Of course, there had been much argument and manoeuvring for position as well as accommodation. Bevan proved to be adroit at exploiting professional divisions, notably by offering concessions to the teaching hospitals and hospital consultants which helped to overcome the opposition of the general practitioners (Forsyth 1966). But in one critical area government made no challenge to professional power. In a speech to the Royal Medico-Psychological Association in 1945, the new Minister articulated a view of the relationship between doctors and the state that was to hold sway right through to the late 1980s: 'I conceive it the function of the Ministry of Health to provide the medical profession with the best and most modern apparatus of medicine and to enable them freely to use it, in accordance with their training, for the benefit of the people of the country. Every doctor must be free to use that apparatus without interference from secular organisations' (quoted by Watkin 1978: 40). Thus the primary NHS legislation was concerned with creating an environment for the delivery of health care by independent practitioners, rather than with regulating the production of medical care itself. In Klein's (1990) memorable phrase, an 'implicit concordat' was forged whereby Ministers would decide on resource levels while clinicians would have autonomy within a given budget.

These three characteristic features of the NHS – the vesting of a duty to provide care in a Minister accountable to Parliament, a unified hospital service managed through a single administrative hierarchy and the institutionalized recognition of professional autonomy – have largely determined the nature of health care regulation in the years since 1948. Taken together they have resulted in an organization split into bureaucratic and professional segments, each with its own regulatory machinery. The powers vested in the Minister of Health (and, latterly, the Secretary of State for Health) provide the basis for a system of bureaucratic regulation of the administrative segment. But since the establishment of the NHS left medical autonomy unimpaired, control of the professional segment of the organization depended on professional self-regulation. These systems of professional control generally pre-date the NHS, although the 1948 Act and subsequent legislation make specific provisions for the delegation of certain responsibilities to the profession. The most important control mechanisms include the capacity of the General Medical Council (GMC) and other professional registration bodies to determine entry to the profession and punish misconduct, the powers of the Royal Colleges and the British Medical Association to investigate allegations of improper behaviour, and the power of the defence societies to refuse to represent a member (Jacob 1988: 157).

Until recently bureaucratic regulation has impinged on the activity of doctors only in certain limited areas. Official inquiries of various kinds, complaints pursued through community health councils, and investigations under the Department of Health's Circular HC81/5 (Health Service Complaints Procedure) may all be concerned with doctors' behaviour (see Jacob and Davies 1987: ss. 022–026). However, power in many of these areas has remained largely in the hands of the medical profession because of its incorporation in key locations within the administrative structure. Thus apart from the many medically qualified staff who hold posts within the NHS management hierarchy, doctors play a key role in the system of advisory and executive committees that exists at regional and district health authority levels. These latter responsibilities are, of course, additional to, and distinct from, the positions held by these same doctors in the medical hierarchy – the functional end of the NHS – which does not stand in a direct line management relationship with the administration.

To the extent that there has been a perceptible growth in health care regulation in the last decade, it has been a reflection of the increasing work done by the central bureaucratic machinery. This machinery brings together control mechanisms which relate to a number of disparate organization functions – policy implementation, strategic planning, some areas of operational management, and also certain aspects of disciplinary action. These different control mechanisms converge in a relatively undifferentiated body of organizational rules and common enforcement structures. Thus from the standpoint of those within the system, the origin of instructions in statute, statutory instrument, Departmental circular or managerial command generally has less practical significance than their content.

THE RESURGENCE OF CENTRALISM

Parliamentary control was a prerequisite for a national, state-financed health service, but it set up a tension between centre and periphery which has yet to be fully resolved (Klein 1989). The vesting in the Health Minister of a duty to provide a comprehensive health service created a constitutional fiction. The Minister became responsible to Parliament for a system which, because of its complexity and dependence on professional expertise, has tended to be resistant to detailed control from the centre.

The organizational fragmentation resulting from the 1948 tripartite structure meant that central control was largely illusory from the start. The 1974 reorganization was intended to tighten hierarchical accountability by creating a clearer chain of command linking the tiers of the service. Its twin themes of integration and managerialism represented an attempt to move closer to an essentially Weberian model of the imperatively co-ordinated bureaucracy, with guidance and instructions from the centre shaping behaviour at the periphery. Yet experience quickly exposed the fallacy of this vision. By 1980 many commentators were concluding that centralism was dead. It had become clear, for example, that government policies to divert resources from the acute sector to the so-called Cinderella services had been subverted by non-compliance and inadequate resourcing. Haywood and Alaszewski (1980) show how policy on service priorities, set out in the 1976 Consultative Document, foundered in the face of local opposition and strong cost pressures in the acute sector. As the decade drew to a close, statements on priorities took on a less prescriptive, more circumscribed tone. For example, in the 1977 Planning Document *The Way Forward*, health authorities were advised that figures set out were 'not specific targets to be reached by declared dates in any locality'. Similarly, Department of Health and Social Security (DHSS)[1] planning guidelines issued in the following year cautioned against regarding expenditure and activity projections as fixed targets, suggesting that they should be seen merely as 'signposts indicating the direction of change' (HC(78)12, para 1.4, quoted by Haywood and Alaszewski 1980: 58).

Largely by default the role of health authorities in relating national priorities to local need had gained official recognition. But a policy that had evolved largely on the basis of pragmatism gained new ideological underpinnings with the election in 1979 of a Conservative government committed to 'rolling back the State'. The Party's manifesto commitment to 'simplify and decentralize the service and cut back bureaucracy' was reflected in a continuing retreat from the expression of priorities in terms of norms or targets. The policies developed under the Conservative Health Secretary, Patrick Jenkin, were to culminate in 1982 in the emergence of new district health authorities, which were intended to exemplify the virtues of localism and devolved authority. At the same time the 'bureaucracy' was pruned through the abolition of the (middle) 'area' tier of the service.

Yet even as the 1982 reorganization was implemented a dramatic policy shift was occurring. Paradoxically, the changed political climate, with its clearer ideological undercurrents, was to herald a return to centralism in a new guise. In centralism 'Mk 2', the focus shifted from service planning to cost containment. Against the background of a strengthening climate of fiscal conservatism, government became concerned to apply new financial disciplines to the public services, and began to develop procedures to tighten financial monitoring and control.

Following the appointment of a new Secretary of State, Norman Fowler, the DHSS embarked on a series of closely co-ordinated initiatives to 'improve accountability' in the NHS (Harrison 1988; Klein 1989).[2] Chief among these were a review process and a set of performance indicators announced in January 1982. The former involved an annual process whereby Ministers were to lead a Departmental review of the long-term plans, objectives and effectiveness of the regions in meetings with regional chairmen and officers. The primary concern of the reviews was to ensure that RHAs were implementing national policy and meeting statutory obligations. Regions in turn were to review the plans and performance of their own districts.

Performance indicators were intended to augment the review progress by facilitating comparisons between districts which would help Ministers and regional chairmen to assess how effectively manpower and other resources were being used. Disquiet about accountability had been growing in government and Parliament more generally. The Public Accounts Committee (PAC) (1980–81), for example, had commented adversely on the DHSS's failure to make inter-regional comparisons, and suggested the need for:

> a flow of information about the activities of the districts which will enable the regions, and in turn the DHSS, to monitor performance effectively and to take necessary action to remedy any serious deficiencies, or inefficiency, which may develop.
>
> (PAC 1980–81: xvii)

The new indicators were to be compulsory and, in the first instance, were to be based on data already routinely collected. They were used experimentally in the review process in the final seven regional reviews in 1982, and the first national 'package' of indicators was introduced in England in September 1983. It contained some seventy indicators relating to clinical work, finance, manpower, support services and estate management. The clinical indicators were not concerned directly with treatment outcomes, but related mainly to resource use in broad specialty groups, using such measures as average length of hospital stay, throughput of patients per bed per annum, and turnover interval of beds. As Harrison (1988: 58) notes, rankings were largely determined by the aggregate behaviour of doctors rather than the decisions of managers.

Other initiatives followed. There was the experimental use of private accountants to audit health authority accounts; the extension of 'Rayner Scrutinies' from the Civil Service to the NHS;[3] the introduction in January 1983 of central control of NHS manpower, and in September a DHSS instruction to health authorities to engage in competitive tendering for laundry, domestic and catering services. This spate of activity culminated in the publication of the findings of an inquiry into NHS management arrangements carried out by a group of prominent businessmen (the Griffiths Report), which we will return to consider later.

The resurgence of centralism in the NHS was the product of several forces. Klein suggests that by 1982, with public expenditure still rising alarmingly, the Conservative government's approach to the management of the public sector shifted: a judgement was taken that the long-term objective of 'less government' might in the short-term imply 'more government'.

> In a sense the Conservative Government can be seen as the equivalent of the Tudor Monarchy asserting the power of the state in order to modernise a country previously dominated by feudal barons and corporate interests like the Church. To disperse the corporate groups that had

created the sclerotic post-war consensus in support of their own interests (as the Tory revivalists saw it), the State had to use its authority to break them. It therefore needed more power, not less.

(Klein 1989: 198)

The change of tack reflected concern over financial management in public administration more generally, rather than any specific preoccupation with the NHS. Initially, its impact was greatest in the central government departments themselves. The NHS reforms of 1982–83 need to be set against this wider public sector management climate, and pressure to spread the new disciplines from the government departments to the public utilities and other areas of state provision. In this latter regard, the parliamentary Public Accounts Committee (PAC) and Social Services Committee played a key role in pressing for more effective control and monitoring of NHS performance, particularly manpower use (Harrison 1988). Increased parliamentary scrutiny of the public services was to be a feature of the 1980s. The development of a state audit system exercised by PAC, the Comptroller and Auditor General and the National Audit Office following the 1983 National Audit Act (Garrett 1986) put the question of managerial efficiency and effectiveness firmly under the spotlight, and helps to explain the preoccupation with 'accountability' as the decade drew to a close.

Central control was crucial both to the implementation and operation of this wider reform movement, but one of the paradoxes of the change process is that it was clothed in a rhetoric of choice, decentralization and efficiency which obscured and denied continuities with the centralism of the past. The new rhetoric argued that bureaucratic regulation could be replaced by the disciplines of market competition, and that the old modes of administration should give way to the more efficient methods of corporate management. Yet while private sector management was the explicit model, change also grew out of an analysis of the maladies of the state bureaucracies with a lineage and precedents of its own.

THE NEW PUBLIC MANAGEMENT

Although the new public sector policies – notably the strong emphasis on cost-containment and use of 'business' models – came to be associated with the philosophy of Thatcherism, they had close parallels with policies that were already reshaping public administration in New Zealand, Australia and Canada, sometimes under Labour governments. Christopher Hood (1990) has coined the term the 'new public management' (NPM) as a convenient shorthand for the administrative doctrines that gained ascendancy at this time. He outlines five loosely linked themes that characterized the new approach.

1 There is a shift of focus from issues of policy to issues of management, generally accompanied by the introduction of formal performance appraisal and the use of measurable efficiency criteria. Lord Rayner, brought in from Marks and Spencer plc by the 1979 Thatcher government to advise on improving the efficiency of government departments, was to recall that 'no one in my time in Whitehall knew in financial management terms how much it cost to run government . . . Ministers, politicians and officials have been mesmerized by the "glamour" of policy; and the costs of administering the policies were regarded as the candle-ends of public expenditure' (Rayner 1984: 2 quoted by Fry 1988: 6). Early moves towards tightening financial management in the Civil Service included the 'Rayner Scrutinies' and the implementation of the Management Information System for Ministers (MINIS)[4] in the Department of the Environment under Michael Heseltine (Likierman 1982). Later these developments were to be 'universalized' to all government departments in the form of the 1982 Financial Management Initiative (FMI) (Fry 1984; 1988), which introduced a model of semi-autonomous Civil Service managers organizing work within prescribed cash limits.

2 While official rhetoric highlights efficiency improvements, the emphasis in practice is on reducing or limiting aggregate expenditure. The Thatcher government's 'grand strategy' for the Civil Service included the wider implementation of the system of cost centres and cash limits associated with MINIS, the chopping back of the career hierarchy, the demise of the central Civil Service Department (with its functions distributed between the Treasury and the Cabinet Office), and an ending of the 'fair comparisons' salary system (Fry 1984). The quest for economy was reflected in a 6.2 per cent reduction in staff numbers in the non-industrial Civil Service in the 1979–82 period.

3 There is increasing recourse to the language and practice of private sector corporate management. This is reflected in a marked shift towards quantified output targets rather than more traditional 'input' or 'process' controls; replacement of traditional career tenure with limited term contracts; reliance on financial incentives (performance-related pay) rather than control through traditional culture or ethos; and greater emphasis on a decentralized freedom of managers to manage, albeit within a framework of increased accountability and closer monitoring. Michael Heseltine, during his time at Environment and Defence, and Rayner and Sir John Ibbs (his successor) at the Efficiency Unit, provided obvious points of contact with the business world. Private sector models were central to the FMI and the further reforms that followed the 1988 Efficiency Unit report, *Improving Management in Government: The Next Steps.*

4 There is a longer-term trend towards organizational disaggregation. One aspect of this process is a shift towards public tendering for activities previously performed 'in house' so as to increase 'contestability'. A second, more radical departure is the break-up of traditional bureaucratic structures into quasi-autonomous operating units, which increasingly deal with one another on a 'user-pays' basis and are often required to compete with other agencies in surrogate markets. One influential early model was the State Owned Enterprises (SOEs) created after 1986 by the Lange government in New Zealand to commercialize certain trading functions previously undertaken by central government departments (Boston 1987).[5] In the British Civil Service, the significant developments took place after 1988 with the appearance of the so-called *Next Steps* agencies (Fry *et al.* 1988), and the restructuring of the service. Smaller core departments remained to service ministers and 'sponsor' policy, but responsibility for policy implementation was transferred to a range of semi-autonomous agencies which might or might not have Crown status.

5 There is a shift away from classical public sector regulation to approaches which promote greater contestability, often by dismantling controls which exclude private sector competitors from markets.

NPM had drawn much of its inspiration from the revival of liberal market theory in economics in the late 1970s, particularly from concepts such as public choice, market and non-market failure, contracting, contestability, transparency and agent/principal relations. Such ideas had their origins in works like Niskanen's (1971) celebrated critique of bureaucracy, which were to become required reading in official policy circles. Hood (1990: 10) identifies a second source of influence in the international scientific management movement – 'much of the thrust of NPM has been a form of "Taylorism with computers" applied to the public services'. In this latter regard, the influence of NPM on the health service in the 1980s had continuities with some of the themes of the 1974 NHS reforms, which had also leaned heavily on managerialist models. But in the intervening years management theory had moved on to emphasize culture and incentives as well as systems and structure (Drucker 1974; Deal and Kennedy 1982; Peters and Waterman 1982; Martin 1983; Schein, 1985).

Generally, NPM has evolved not as a co-ordinated strategy, but as a series of diverse and sometimes individualistic initiatives which have developed from a shared analysis of the ills of the contemporary state bureaucracies. In most cases the five characteristics described above have not been taken forward at the same pace. Attention has turned first to new organizational structures, management systems, financial control mechanisms and incentive arrangements, and it is only later that the focus has shifted to the more radical possibilities of organizational disaggregation and the dismantling of controls to allow greater contestability and competition: there has generally been a time lag between 'phase I' and 'phase II' reforms. That was the pattern in the British Civil Service with the progression from the FMI to the *Next Steps*, and the NHS reforms of 1982–91 followed a similar sequence.

FROM GENERAL MANAGEMENT TO THE INTERNAL MARKET

For most of the 1980s government was preoccupied with what we might term the first phase of NPM. Thus the Griffiths reforms[6] – like the Fowler initiatives already mentioned – were concerned in large part with creating clearer lines of managerial accountability, particularly in the financial sphere. The chain of command was simplified by the abolition of the old-style 'consensus management' teams, and the appointment of general managers at regional, district and unit level, charged with overall responsibility for performance within their managerial units. District treasurers' departments were reorganized to give individual units a financial accounting capability, thus paving the way for the introduction of unit budgets and the extension of financial disciplines to the lowest level of the administrative hierarchy.[7] To this end arrangements were made for treasurers' departments to work with unit management to determine virement rules, spending limits, and the relationship between unit budgets and district-wide budgets for functional services. Along with increased accountability, the Griffiths Report had emphasized the need for greater management freedoms and personal incentives. After 1986 individual performance review and performance-related pay were introduced for senior officers, now increasingly appointed on short-term contracts.

The preoccupation with 'first phase' reforms continued up to 1988. The Review Process first introduced under Norman Fowler was extended to apply to all levels of the service, and modified at regional level to introduce meetings between the NHS Management Board and regional officers at which progress in planning and cost-improvement programmes were discussed. In 1988 the NHS planning system was reorganized, with the introduction of a new timetable intended to facilitate improved co-ordination of annual district and regional plans ('short-term plans') for service developments and resource allocation, and the associated annual performance reports.

Yet by early 1988 after a winter of highly publicized bed closures and with a new funding crisis looming, it was clear that the first phase of general management had not solved basic problems of resourcing and inefficiency. Progress in implementing management budget systems (Pollitt *et al*. 1988) and quality assurance (Shaw 1986b) had been disappointing. Greater managerial accountability had only served to highlight a fundamental organizational paradox: although pressure could be exerted on the managers who had nominal responsibility for budgets, those managers had little authority over the doctors who created overspends. A King's Fund Institute Briefing Paper, intended to contribute to the debate on health finance towards the end of 1988, put the matter thus:

> the most important consideration is that doctors do not usually have responsibility for budgets in the NHS, nor are they always provided with information about the resource consequences of their decisions. There is a gap between clinicians whose decisions on whom and how to treat largely determine the use of resources, and managers who have overall responsibility for controlling budgets and keeping within resource limits.
>
> (King's Fund 1988: 17)

Like the American hospitals described by the economist John Harris (1977), the NHS might be said to comprise two 'firms', each with its own objectives, managers, pricing structure and constraints. The difficulty was that while there was an emergent process of monitoring and control associated with the budgetary process at the administrative level, similar external mechanisms did not exist to monitor and control clinical practice. In many district health authorities cost-containment problems arose primarily in the acute hospitals, and were largely attributable to factors – such as the unfunded growth of specialty activity and use of more expensive technologies, including investigations, pharmaceuticals and prostheses – over which managers had little control.

The perceived need to bring clinicians within the same framework of accountability as managers was a central issue in the Prime Ministerial Review of the NHS announced in February 1988. The options considered for more radical reform of the service included steps of the kind already implemented elsewhere in the public sector – what we might term 'phase II' NPM reforms. But the split organization of the NHS, with its administrative and professional segments, posed special problems which necessarily had to be addressed within any overall reform package. Only in education had similar problems previously been encountered, and a partial precedent set out in the provisions of the Education Reform Act 1988 for schools to opt out of local authority control.[8] However, the NHS required its own innovative solutions.

The White Paper, *Working for Patients* (Department of Health 1989a) (henceforth *WFP*), that emerged from the NHS Review combined NPM-type proposals for disaggregation and increased competition with a number of measures which addressed the power of the doctors. The central thrust of the reforms, now incorporated in the National Health Service and Community Care Act 1990, is to replace the present bureaucratically regulated NHS planning and resource allocation system with an internal market in health care.[9] The lower tiers of the administrative hierarchy have been rejigged to create a clearer separation between purchasers and providers of services. While district health authorities (DHAs) will be accountable for the financial and operational management of some units, they will concentrate increasingly on a service purchasing role. Larger general practices may also exercise such a role by applying to hold special NHS 'funds' which can be used to buy services from either NHS or private hospitals. On the provider side, organizational units below district level are free to apply for National Health Service Trust (NHST) status and move outside the central management structure (though remaining nominally within the NHS). At the same time steps are being taken to encourage oo operation with the independent sector, and ensure that it can compete with NHS hospitals on fair terms. DHAs and GPs will purchase services by placing contracts with a range of competing providers, hospitals remaining under DHA management, NHSTs and the independent sector.

The establishment of NHSTs with substantial devolved authority over operational matters amounts to a significant decoupling of provider units from the present integrated health service. Fifty-seven units gained approval for transfer to NHST status in April 1991; many more are expected to follow the 'first wave'. Each trust will be run by a board of directors and will have certain freedoms not available to units remaining under NHS management, as well as specific powers and duties. They will be able to acquire and dispose of assets, borrow, retain an operating surplus in normal circumstances, determine their own management structures, decide their own staffing arrangements and policy, and advertise their services (Department of Health 1989d). Trusts have powers to enter contracts with both NHS and independent bodies, to commission research and provide training, to charge private patients for accommodation, and to generate income through permitted commercial activities.[10]

A number of steps are being taken to improve 'contestability'. DHAs will be required to pay interest on capital assets (1990 Act s. 19(4)), so as to 'place NHS hospitals on a more level footing with private hospitals, which have to meet the cost of capital on a normal, commercial basis' (*WFP:* 9.9).[11] Further encouragement was given to the private sector when the government introduced provisions in the 1989 Finance Act granting income tax relief on private insurance premiums for those aged 60 and over. Government has let it be known that it expects the volume of clinical work contracted by the NHS to the private sector to increase, and also to see a growth in joint ventures between providers in the two sectors. As noted above, NHSTs are empowered to provide accommodation and services for private patients. The 1990 Act (s. 25) confers similar freedoms on directly managed units by removing the requirement for formal Department of Health authorization before private schemes can be initiated.

Even more important in our view, however, is the impact of the reforms on medical autonomy. It has been a remarkable feature of the NHS that clinicians have been largely isolated from financial pressures, certainly in the sense that their remuneration and that of their employing institution are unrelated to the volume and quality of clinical activity (Pollitt 1987). The 1983 Griffiths proposals to replace consensus management with general managers and to involve clinicians in management budgeting began to challenge this state of affairs; but the 1990–91 reforms go much further. The detailed provisions affecting doctors fall into five main areas: the extension of clinical management; compulsory participation in medical audit; introduction of new-style consultant contracts; reform of distinction awards; and the introduction of indicative prescribing budgets.

The expansion of clinical management builds on the Resource Management Initiative (RMI), that evolved out of the Griffiths proposals for management budgets. By 1989 the full RMI process had been implemented in something over twenty acute units, and the White Paper set out plans to extend this to 260 units by April 1992 (*WFP*: 16). The intention is that doctors themselves become more closely involved in managing the effective use of resources within the parameters set by general managers, and that information necessary for costing and evaluating clinical procedures becomes available to management at all levels. While many commentators have welcomed this development, there are warnings that it should not be seen as a panacea; that problems with the RMI and the strength of medical resistance may not have been acknowledged (for example, see Pollitt *et al.* 1988); that the reforms are being introduced in advance of the results of an independent evaluation of RMI which the Department of Health is supporting; and that the government's timetable is over-optimistic (Harrison *et al.* 1989).

A requirement to participate in medical audit will be included in consultants' contracts and GPs' terms of service. At face value medical audit is a professionally led initiative to analyse and monitor the quality of care, but it remains unclear how far quality issues overlap with cost-effectiveness issues and how managers will interpret their role in the process. As a recent Department of Health Working Paper indicates: 'management too has significant responsibility for seeing that resources are used in the most effective way, and will therefore need to ensure that an effective system of medical audit is in place' (Department of Health 1989b: para 3.3). This implies a degree of managerial influence over the content of audit systems. Moreover, where management is not satisfied that resources are being used effectively, it will be able to initiate an independent audit, which may take the form of 'external peer review or a joint professional and managerial appraisal of a particular service'(Department of Health 1989b: para 3.2). The new arrangements for audit are likely to accelerate the shift towards formal performance measurement. Thus a recent Social Services Committee report on the reforms expressed the hope that 'the Audit Commission in conjunction with the relevant professional bodies and Royal Colleges will succeed in developing a methodology for assessing outcomes in health care' (Social Services Committee 1988–89). If such measures do emerge, clinical guidelines linked to the treatment packages that are bought and sold may not be far behind.

The changes in consultants' contracts, job descriptions and appointments mean that management will have a greater role in defining the duties and responsibilities of post-holders, and will be in a position to monitor performance against contractual obligations. District general managers will take a more active role in the appointments procedure, which to date has been seen to be controlled by the medical profession, and will need to approve the content of contracts which set out the scope and extent of each consultant's duties more explicitly than in the past. Similar trends are discernible in the changes made to the system of distinction awards to reward professional excellence. The criteria for basic 'C' awards will be modified to take account not only of clinical skills but also commitment to 'the management and development of the service', and the composition of selection committees (which at present are solely professional) will be modified to give significant representation to general managers (Department of Health 1989f).

The introduction of indicative prescribing budgets reflects the Department of Health's long-standing concern that the wide variation in Family Practitioner Committees' prescribing costs arises from wasteful prescribing by some GPs. Government has made provisions to allocate each regional health authority (RHA) a firm budget from which they will allocate drug budgets to Family Health Service Authorities (FHSAs)[12] within the region, who will in turn be responsible for allocating *indicative* drug budgets to GPs in their areas. Allocations to RHAs and FHSAs will initially reflect existing spending patterns, but there will be a gradual change to a weighted capitation formula. FHSAs are expected to establish policies for allocating funds to practices which will take into account capitation, but also local social and epidemiological factors and special factors, such as the needs of particular patients for unusually expensive drugs. The intention is to 'bring downward pressure on those practices which are above average [in cost]' (Department of Health 1989e). It is emphasized that patients will always get the medicines they need, but FHSAs will be able to impose sanctions on overspending doctors, possibly through withholding remuneration. Legislation was necessary to effect some of these reforms, and section 18 of the 1990 Act requires FHSAs to specify 'indicative amounts' to GPs, and defines 'practice' for these purposes. Its main significance is that there is now a statutory requirement for GPs to 'seek to secure' that the cost of prescribing on drugs and appliances in any financial year does not exceed the amount fixed by the FHSA, except with consent and for good reasons (s. 18(4)). Indicative budgets may therefore be expected to have a considerably greater impact than the limited prescribing list introduced in 1986.

Although none of these developments amounts in itself to a frontal challenge to medical authority, their cumulative effect will be to enhance the power of the manager *vis-à-vis* the clinician. Taken collectively the measures represent a twofold strategy. The new consultant contracts, the reform of distinction awards and indicative prescribing amounts may be seen as attempts to augment direct external control over clinicians by managers. Clinical management and medical audit, on the other hand, seek to shift the focus of professional self-regulation to take more account of quality issues and to assimilate doctors into a managerialist culture. It is therefore a strategy with both Weberian and Durkheimian overtones: administrative and professional segments will be brought closer together both through imperative controls associated with the greater formalization of employment terms and practice guidelines (in the area of prescribing), and through normative controls, in the form of efforts to promote common perspectives which pay greater attention to resource use.

However, more important than these specific developments may be the overall impact of provider competition on clinical behaviour. Though the reforms stop short of placing hospital doctors in the market place as independent contractors, many will find themselves located in units which face strong competitive pressures. To the extent that real competition occurs, inefficient hospitals will go out of business. Although one may suspect that this eventuality will be as unrealistic in political terms under the new system as it is at present, the rhetoric of cost-containment is likely to exert a powerful influence. Doctors will need to reconcile treatments with the packages of care sold by managers or risk putting their employing organization in a loss-making situation. The processes of costing and treatment specification associated with the contracting process itself are therefore likely to make significant inroads into the clinical freedom of doctors, which will be difficult to resist without seeming to place the economic viability of the provider unit in doubt. Certainly the experience of the North American system suggests that competitive contracting and the associated use of diagnosis-related groups (DRGs) has significantly eroded clinical autonomy for individual doctors (Light and Levine 1988).

REGULATING THE MARKET PLACE

The three characteristic features of the 1948 NHS outlined earlier in the chapter – institutionalized medical autonomy, the rejection of organizational pluralism, and central control through powers vested in the Secretary of State – all appear at odds with a shift from bureaucratic to market regulation. In this sense, the 1990–91 reforms appear to signal a decisive break with the old order. Yet while the 'internal market' does, in our view, represent a real challenge to professional power and NHS integration, the retreat from central planning implied by the market metaphor is by no means synonymous with a diminution of central power. *Working for Patients* puts much emphasis on the desirability of decentralization of decision-making: 'as much power and responsibility as possible will be delegated to local level' (*WFP*: 1.9). Proponents of the reforms suggest that management within the new NHSTs, and even those units remaining under DHA management, will have more autonomy with respect to operational decision-making than in the past. However, the greater freedom of managers to manage will be accompanied by increased emphasis on accountability and performance review. In practice, therefore, it may amount to a rather spurious autonomy, extended only so long as the decisions of local managers remain in line with policy objectives and financial targets set from above.

In fact, alongside some measure of devolution of decision-making authority, there will be a perceptible strengthening of managerial controls at all levels. In this respect the broad changes set in train by the 1983 Griffiths Report continue. A new NHS Policy Board, chaired and appointed by the Secretary of State, will determine strategy, objectives and finances for the service in the light of government policy, and will oversee the work of the NHS Management Executive. This latter body, headed by a chief executive, will deal with all operational matters within the policy and strategy set by the Policy Board. It will exercise authority over slimmed-down RHAs, which will concentrate more than at present on monitoring performance and assessing effectiveness. The chain of command will continue down to the DHAs – the purchasers of health care for their resident populations. The traditional separation of general practice from the central management hierarchy, which dates back to the tripartite division of the 1948 NHS, will finally be ended. The Family Health Service Authorities (which replace the existing Family Practitioner Committees) are placed in a management relationship with RHAs, which parallels the relationship between RHAs and DHAs (s. 12), and includes their activities within the ambit of the new NHS Executive. In words that echo the Grey Book (Department of Health and Social Security 1972),[13] *Working for Patients* states that: 'The overall effect of these changes will be to introduce for the first time a clear and effective chain of management command running from Districts through Regions to the Chief Executive and from there to the Secretary of State' (*WFP*: 2.6).

The new management arrangements are predicated on the assumption that it is possible to achieve a clear distinction at national level 'between the policy responsibilities of Ministers and the operational responsibilities of the Chief Executive and top management' (*WFP*: 1.17). The separation of policy-making and operational management functions has, of course, been a constant theme of successive NHS reorganizations back to 1974. A distinction at the Minister/chief executive level was central to the 1983 Griffiths management model but, although briefly attempted in the 1980s, was abandoned when the Health Minister became Chairman of the Management Board (see Harrison *et al.* 1989). It seems unlikely, given the multifarious financial and political pressures on the Secretary of State from Parliament and other Departments, that this separation will prove to be more sustainable now.

This brings us to an even more critical area: the powers delegated to the Health Secretary and the issue of how far the creation and operation of the *internal market* itself depends on central executive power. The inescapable need for government intervention, even within a market-based system, was a problem that health economists had foreseen:

> The natural inclination of a competitive market is for it to become monopolistic. Thus Enthoven *advocates legislation* to ensure that consumers are offered an effective choice of insurers annually. . . . The liberal-marketeers admit a role for the state as 'policeman of the market place' who protects the competitive process. It is likely that the role would be extensive and executed with some difficulty in the health care market.
>
> (Maynard 1988: 151, emphasis in original)

What was less easy to anticipate was the extent of the conceptual gymnastics needed to sustain the market metaphor in the NHS. The two entities central to the 'internal' market are the NHS contract and the NHS Trust (the subjects respectively of sections 4 and 5 of the 1990 Act). Ostensibly, the establishment of semi-autonomous trusts represents a strategy for ensuring increased provider competition, while the NHS contract defines the new more 'business-like' relationships that will characterize the reorganized system. Yet both highlight the crucial role of central power in ensuring that the quasi-market becomes a working reality.

The NHS contract represents a radical departure from the traditional concept of contract as a voluntary agreement through which parties make legally binding promises (Hughes and Dingwall 1990a). Given that there are substantial constraints on DHAs regarding when and where[14] to let NHS contracts, they have more of the characteristics of an 'imposed contract' than a freely entered agreement. Moreover, since disputes will be resolved through (internal) arbitration rather than through recourse to the courts, they are not legally enforceable in the usual sense. The Health Secretary is given a critical role in dispute resolution: he 'may determine the matter himself or, if he considers it appropriate, appoint a person to consider and determine it in accordance with regulations' (1990 Act, s. 4(5)). In fact, these powers seem to go well beyond what a conventional arbitration role would require. The Secretary of State has authority to deal not only with disputes over alleged breach (s. 4(3)), but also disputes arising out of negotiations over the terms of a proposed contract (s. 4(4)). Since the Secretary can specify terms to be included in a proposed contract and direct that it is proceeded with (s. 4(6)), he can effectively impose a contract. With regard to disputes over existing contracts, the Secretary may vary terms of an agreement or bring it to an end (s. 4(7)). He is empowered to impose 'directions' (including directions regarding payments) needed to give effect to variation or termination, and these are to be treated as if they were the result of agreement between the parties themselves. The overall effect is to place with the executive powers considerably greater than those traditionally available to judges in contract cases, and to blur the distinction between administrative and legal controls.

The Secretary of State is cast in a similarly exaggerated 'policeman of the market' role with respect to trusts (Hughes and Dingwall 1990b; Hughes 1991). While the White Paper emphasizes independence and enhanced rights, the open-ended nature of the 1990 legislation means that the NHST is subject to a degree of direct government control that no ordinary trust or corporation experiences. Thus the Health Secretary may give the NHST such functions as he may specify, and he may determine the membership of trust boards and the form of proceedings (1990 Act, ss. 5(5), 5(7)). NHSTs must achieve the financial objectives set by the Secretary with the consent of the Treasury (s. 10(2)). They must comply with the Health Secretary's directions on such matters as officers' qualifications, their appointment and employment, the retention of assets, and (subject to certain caveats) with directions and circulars to health authorities (Sched 2, para 6(2)). With respect to the financing of NHSTs, the Secretary is empowered to regulate the terms and upper limits of borrowing, and he may direct the transfer of monies judged to be surplus to requirements to the Exchequer (Sched 3, paras 1(60), 3(1), 6). Finally, where deemed necessary the Secretary may dissolve an NHST and transfer its assets to another body. In many instances these powers will remain unused but, clearly, formidable controls exist if problems arise.

AN OVERVIEW

With the apparent breakdown of the post-war consensus, the mechanisms that regulated resource allocation and policy implementation in the old NHS are being swept away. The rise of new policies of disaggregation and deregulation to promote 'contestability' seem certain to create a more pluralistic health care system. At the same time government has mounted a concerted challenge to medical power, both by encouraging a change in the focus of professional self-regulation, and shifting the frontiers of bureaucratic regulation so that it impinges more directly on clinical practice. In organizational terms, the recent reforms represent, at different levels, both a search for greater system integration and a decoupling of functional units. There is a move to bring professional and administrative segments closer together and rationalize management structures, at just the time when provider units are offered semi-autonomous status. Indeed – as we argued above – the decoupling of NHSTs and the shift to greater provider competition are seen as an important factor in exposing managers and clinicians to common pressures and incentives.

This is not to say that bureaucratic regulation has been supplanted by the market. In the aftermath of the 1990 Act, and with a general election looming, post-Thatcher Conservatism has drawn away from the more radical metaphors of the White Paper. A new Secretary of State, William Waldegrave, has let it be known that the business language had been 'overdone', and that health care is not simply a market commodity. Yet in a deeper sense the 'internal market' has never been compatible with a shift to a full-blown market system. Its operation in crucial areas depends on just the exercise of central power that is the antithesis of *laissez-faire* competition. In this respect the internal market, like the older bureaucratic machinery it replaces, has been shaped by the 1948 system. Although the vision of an integrated service and the original bargain with the clinicians may be crumbling, parliamentary accountability and the associated delegation of powers to the Health Secretary have proved more enduring. Critics of the 1990 Act were not slow to point to the frequency with which the phrase 'Secretary of State' occurred in the statute and the wide scope of

Ministerial discretion.[15] In longer-term perspective, the significant feature of the 1990 Act may be that it extended Bevan's vision of a Ministerial duty of provision in ways that he had never envisaged.

If Klein (1989: 198) was right to argue that the liberal-marketeers reached a judgement that they needed more rather than less state power if they were to sweep away the 'sclerotic post-war consensus', that may have been a fundamental miscalculation. Power once granted is not easily relinquished. The likely consequence of the 1990–91 reforms is that bureaucratic regulation will live on, but with the loci of power shifted towards the top (the Health Secretary and the NHS Management Executive) rather than the middle tiers of the management hierarchy (the regions). This will be the necessary counterbalance to a growth of self-protective behaviour and unfair practices at the provider level. As a result the internal market risks delivering the worst of both worlds: the complications of the quasi-market and the rigidities of continuing, partially disguised, top-down control.

NOTES

1 North American readers may be confused by the changing terminology. The old Ministry of Health was subsumed in the merged Department of Health and Social Security (DHSS) in 1968. However, twenty years later health and social security again split and the Department of Health was created.

2 Admittedly, the trend towards tighter financial control was not wholly new. In 1976, against the background of historically high levels of inflation, NHS planning in volume terms had given way to planning within cash limits. Moreover, the resource allocation process itself had become increasingly formalized following the acceptance of the findings of the Resource Allocation Working Party in the same year. But the initiatives of 1982 represented a move by the centre for the first time to intervene in detail in financial management at the periphery (see Harrison 1988).

3 Early in the life of the Thatcher government, Sir Derek (later Lord) Rayner, Chairman of Marks and Spencer plc was appointed to advise on efficiency and the elimination of waste in government departments. The Rayner Scrutinies involved the secondment of a senior officer from another department to advise on efficiency in some designated area of activity. In the NHS areas selected for attention included vacancy advertising, storage of supplies, catering costs and NHS residential property.

4 MINIS is a method for improving control and information in government departments. As originally applied in the Department of the Environment, the system collects information on activities in a way which helps Ministers to take decisions on priorities, and review performance in implementing objectives and effectiveness. It involves a detailed specification of responsibility for departmental functions, and a common procedure for costing the operations of the department. A MINIS 'round' involves a systematic comparison of performance in three time periods, including a 'retrospective' period, the period in which the round occurs and a future planned performance period. For a detailed account, see Likierman 1982.

5 There are a number of reasons why many of the pioneering steps in NPM should have occurred in New Zealand: state-owned enterprises accounted for more than 12 per cent of GDP in the early 1980s; the efficiency of the public sector was critical because growth had been low by international standards; the NZ Treasury had been much influenced by market-liberal philosophy, particularly its modern reinterpretations; and under the first Lange government, at least, there was considerable political resistance to a shift to full-blown privatization (see Boston 1987).

6 For a fuller account of the Griffiths reforms, see Harrison 1988; Petchey 1986; and Klein 1990.

7 Progress in implementing management budgets was slow and at the time of writing has been implemented only in a limited number of experimental projects, mainly in acute hospitals, under the umbrella of the Resource Management Initiative. The acceleration of RMI is one of the central planks of the reform package associated with the 1990 Act.

8 Sir George Young, in debate in the House of Commons, was to observe that: 'The parallels between the reforms in this [Act] and those in the Education Reform Act are striking. . . . For example, the proposals for grant-maintained schools are replicated by those for self-governing hospitals, giving a measure of independence and local autonomy within the state-funded sector. Those for local management of schools are replicated by those for general practitioners to become fund holders, allocating resources as closely as possible to the point of consumption. The proposals for open enrolment and funds following the pupil . . . are paralleled by those that facilitate switching one's GP and greater reliance on capitation, so rewarding popular provision and making the system more responsive to the consumer. National curriculum and assessment are paralleled by the proposals for medical audit to try to measure output and value for money, to raise standards and to determine where improvements might be made' (H.C. Deb, vol. 163, col. 527).

9 For a fuller account of the reforms introduced by the 1990 Act, see Hughes 1991.

10 See 1990 Act, Schedule 2, paras 10, 11, 12, 14, 15.

11 The capital charging scheme will apply to NHSTs as well as to other NHS bodies. However, the originating capital debt of a trust will be divided between an interest-bearing loan and public dividend capital (PDC). The latter carries no fixed repayment obligations but is expected in the long run to yield dividends at least equal to the interest that would have been paid. The possibility of deferring payment with respect to PDC has been seen by some critics as one of the major financial advantages of NHSTs over directly managed units.

12 Following the 1990 Act the old FPCs will be revamped as FHSAs.

13 Management Arrangements for the Reorganized National Health Service (Department of Health and Social Security, 1972, para 1.5(e).

14 Although the original proposals for DHAs to specify a range of 'core services' that providers would be required to offer locally have been watered down, there is still a clear *de facto* necessity to ensure that certain services are available in the area, and consequently a necessity to place certain contracts with providers who may have a local monopoly.

15 One of the more telling contributions to the Second Reading debate in Parliament was made by the opposition health spokesman when he noted that 'Secretary of State' came up 127 times in the Bill (not counting references to

Scotland), and that the Secretary alone was empowered to lay orders and give instructions: 'I understand,' he went on,'that it is fashionable to describe this arrangement as enabling legislation. This is a misuse of our language. It is a Bill for arbitrary government by whomever happens to be Secretary of State at the time' (H.C. Deb, vol. 163, col. 515, 7 December 1989).

6 The pragmatic management of error and the antecedents of disputes over the quality of medical care

Stephen Daniels

The Chairman of the Department of Surgery at Gulfview Medical Centre (GC)[1] has frequently remarked before various audiences that there are probably three errors per patient per nursing shift in their burn unit. If there are three shifts per day, he says, that means nine errors per patient per day; and with an average stay of about twenty days in the unit, that adds up to one hundred and eighty errors per patient per stay! This, he notes, is in addition to a mortality rate of about 20 per cent. Whether the Chairman's estimate of the amount of medical error in the burn unit is reasonably accurate, or could ever be verified, is not the important issue. The story's point is his working assumption, one generally shared within the medical profession, that medicine is an inexact science. While the goal may be perfection, health care professionals must deal with the fact that errors are inevitable in their work. In short, medical work is highly error prone (see Paget 1988: 20–7).

Such a view of error in medical work immediately raises questions about the quality of care and treatment; about the accountability of those providing care and treatment; and about the mechanisms for ensuring quality and accountability. In the United States, it also brings to mind the ongoing controversy over medical malpractice litigation as a mechanism for ensuring quality and accountability since errors (or at least perceived errors) are the raw materials for malpractice disputes. The Chairman's anecdote, however, raises an even more fundamental set of issues with regard to the antecedents of such disputes: what is this inevitable occurrence called 'error' for a given set of medical workers; why is it inevitable for their working situation; and how is it handled pragmatically? Answering these questions will better enable us to understand why disputes over the quality of medical care arise. Or more accurately, why so few formal disputes arise in the face of the pervasiveness of error in medical work.[2]

Answering these questions requires a first-hand examination of what can be called the pragmatic management of error within specific work units.

Each work unit within the hospital can be seen as a semi-autonomous social field, an arena that 'can generate rules and customs and symbols internally, but is also vulnerable to rules and decisions and other forces emanating from the larger world by which it is surrounded' (Moore 1973: 720). Each work unit possesses, more or less, its own system of rules, customs and procedures for dealing with the inevitability of error – its own organizational culture (see Ott 1989). Exploring such a social field with regard to the handling of mistakes requires the first-hand examination of medical work and errors as they occur and unfold, rather than a retrospective analysis of patient records, incident reports and other archival materials. This takes us to the very origin of a series of events that could – but seldom does – evolve into a dispute over the quality of medical care. It means studying what Strauss *et al.* (1985: 242) call 'error work' – 'the various tasks involved in preventing, minimizing, defining, detecting, covering up, rectifying, estimating the consequences of . . . mistakes'. The patterns of such work that can be observed within a given unit will reflect the operative meaning of error.

This same point was made in a more practical vein by the surgeon in charge of GC's burn unit, Dr Marrone, in an early discussion about this study. In talking about abstract, a priori definitions of medical error and the potential for quantifying the amount and nature of error, he took issue with the idea of someone coming into his unit with a set definition of error in order to count 'errors' in some nice and neat fashion. As Marrone emphatically put it:

> You won't get anywhere with this. It won't tell you anything because you don't understand what goes on in the unit. You don't understand what error means to these people and what they actually do about it. You really won't be able to understand and assess the amount of error in a unit like this unless you come in and live in the unit so you know what's going on.

This chapter focuses on three things that are important for understanding error and its management: the nature of medical work; the organization of work; and the labelling of events as errors. To understand what error – mistakes at work – means, we need to explore the way in which medical workers see their work. We also need to explore the organization of work on the every-day level because it reflects, in a more concrete form, the way in which work and error are conceptualized. In examining the way in which medical work is seen and organized we find, as Dr Marrone's comments above suggest, that error is not a phenomenon with a precise substantive meaning of general application. It is very much an existential phenomenon whose meaning is based on work that falls short of expectations (both technically and normatively) but depends on the idiosyncrasies of particular patients and situations. Because a precise definition cannot be stated in the abstract, we are directed, instead, to the process in which some actual events that occur in the course of medical work are *labelled* as 'errors'.

To explore these issues, I spent fifteen months observing day-to-day activities of the full range of medical workers (from attending physicians to the aides and janitors) in two surgical intensive care units (one a burn unit and the other a general surgical intensive care unit) in a major urban teaching hospital. This included observing their handling of error.[3] For part of this time, I was assisted by a recent medical school graduate who helped with technical matters. We had full, twenty-four-hour access to the units, access to patient charts, access to unit and staff meetings, and access to rounds and mortality and morbidity meetings. After gaining a working understanding of the units – their organization and staffing, the nature of their work and their major mechanisms for monitoring work – I concentrated our efforts on those parts of the daily or weekly routine where problems and the subject of error were regularly discussed in the context of individual patients.[4] This work was supplemented in two ways. First, I had numerous informal discussions and interviews (over innumerable cups of coffee) with those working in the units concerning their activities and particular errors. Second, I continued to make frequent observations (at different times during the day and night) of the regular work routine in the units.

UNCERTAINTY AND THE NATURE OF MEDICAL WORK

From the day-to-day perspective of the GC medical workers I observed, medical work within the hospital is structured by two key factors: what is seen as the uncertain and contingent nature of medical work itself (see Fox 1980), and the ways in which medical work is consequently organized along with the organizational dynamics characterizing the work environment. Understanding how these things structure medical work on a day-to-day basis is the key to understanding how the GC people view error and how they manage it.[5] These two factors provide the immediate parameters within which these medical workers – from their perspective – must work. Neither the nature of medical work nor its organization is perceived as changing significantly in the short run, so each must be dealt with as best one can. The notion that both of these may change in the long run is irrelevant to GC people as they deal with the day-to-day contingencies of their work.

The nature of medical work is the more important of the two fixed parameters for the GC people. It is the perceived nature of medical work that makes impossible a generally applicable definition of error. Medicine is seen as an inexact science, and is portrayed as problematic, complex and subtle in its practice. Medical workers must regularly deal with the contingencies resulting from the uncertainties inherent in this imperfect and pragmatic science. These problems are compounded by the additional contingencies that accompany the unique histories and situations of individual patients. Consequently, as the Chairman seeks to show with his account of the burn unit, errors are inevitable and even frequent. This is especially true in the critical care arena – perhaps the most uncertain arena in medical work. Because uncertainty is inherent in medical work, error cannot be eliminated. It can, however, be minimized and controlled to a large degree, the Chairman claims.

This idea of the inevitability of error appears throughout the sociological and ethnographic literature on medicine and other occupations. Mistakes are inevitable in all types of work, as are disputes over the quality of work, whether we are talking about medicine or the building trades. Writing in 1951, in an essay entitled 'Mistakes at Work,' Everett C. Hughes said: 'Occupations, considered as bundles of skills, are subject to the contingencies of learning and of maintaining skill, and correlatively, subject to variations in the probability that one will sometimes make mistakes' (1951: 320–1). He also noted that the mistakes for some occupations can be more fateful than others (Hughes 1951: 321). In medicine, of course, the mistakes can be uniquely fateful for patients. As Millman reminds us, 'the risks of medical work are very high; mistakes made in the line of duty may cost a human life' (1977: 91).

Much of the literature that does touch on uncertainty, the inevitability of error and the handling of error comes out of the study of professions and discusses these matters from the perspective of a professional dominance theory. Perhaps the most influential of these professional dominance theorists is Eliot Freidson. His starting point is the idea 'that the separate worlds of experience and reference of the layman and the professional worker are always in potential conflict with each other' (1989: 16–17). Notions like the inevitability of error and uncertainty, from this perspective, are simply devices used to 'normalize' mistakes and thereby allow doctors to avoid accountability.[6] Such ideas are often discussed in a strident, judgemental and highly critical tone. According to Millman, who also writes from this perspective, any occupation that entails risk 'will construct collective rationalizations and defences to help them through their mistakes and to protect themselves from the reactions of the lay world' (1977: 90). Such defences – like the idea of uncertainty – are used to 'neutralize' mistakes. By this Millman means 'the various processes by which medical mistakes are systematically ignored, justified, or made to appear unim-

portant or inconsequential by the doctors who have made them or those
who have noticed that they have been made' (1977: 91). Every aspect of
medical work, she argues, is shaped by a 'collusion' among doctors 'to
ignore and justify errors' (1977: 91).[7]

Such a professional dominance perspective, Marianne Paget notes,
effectively denies the reality for medical workers of the inevitability of
error by casting it as an elaborate excuse to maintain occupational control
and privilege against the lay world (1988: 17–20). It ignores a distinction
made some years ago between ' "real" uncertainty as a clinical and a
scientific phenomenon and the uses to which uncertainty – real or
pretended, "functional" uncertainty – lends itself in the management of
patients and their families' (Davis 1960: 41). The fact that the idea of
uncertainty may be used to 'manage' patients and families does not deny
the existence – in the minds of medical workers – of error as a day-to-day
clinical fact that must be dealt with.

Additionally, the professional dominance perspective misperceives the
way in which medical workers view what they do and how they view error.
It assumes, Bosk notes, 'that what counts as an error is a relatively straightforward matter' and that 'physicians can and should apply a standard
criterion in identifying error' (1979: 23). This presumes, of course, a fairly
precise, detailed and predictable body of knowledge applied to essentially
fungible patients. In fact, Bosk argues that much of this literature does not
address at all the issue of what counts as an error; but rather simply assumes
a degree of objective certainty that makes errors obvious when they occur.[8]
In contrast, as he suggests, the medical worker's view of error is quite
different. And to one interested in the antecedents of disputes between
medical workers and lay people over the quality of care, the medical
worker's view of error is fundamental.

Uncertainty is a day-to-day possibility for the medical workers I observed, an existential reality pervading everything they do. This makes it
difficult, if not impossible, for them to state in advance a set of criteria
providing a substantive definition of error that is generally applicable.
Whenever I asked for a general definition of error, the GC people – not just
the physicians – emphasized this point again and again. Indeed, if I pushed
someone for a general definition my request was likely to be met with a
bewildered shrug.[9] Error only has meaning in real-life situations, and it is
the situations which dictate the meaning of error in any substantial sense.

A particularly graphic illustration of the uncertainty and contingency
that characterized much of what I observed comes from the burn unit and
two separate family conferences conducted by Dr Marrone, the unit's head.
These conferences show how the idea of uncertainty can be used in managing a patient's family (to manage or defuse an incipient dispute) while

still being a clinical reality for medical workers. The second of the two also shows how expectations about the nature of medical work can differ between the lay world and the medical world. The conferences involved two patients admitted to the unit a few days before. Both patients were about forty years old and both had experienced life-threatening burn injuries.

Dr Marrone talked to the Smith family in a conference room inside the burn unit itself. This family was black and poor, and they were frightened. In talking with them Dr Marrone explained the nature and extent of Jesse Smith's injuries, as well as the nature of burn injuries generally and their treatment. He added that Jesse was on a respirator because she had suffered injury to her lungs from inhaling the smoke in addition to the burns. This was a serious problem in itself. The best situation for recovery, Marrone explained, was for younger people in good health. Jesse was not that old, he said – in her late thirties – but she suffered from hypertension which complicated matters, especially with her inhalation injury. In response to Dr Marrone's inquiry, the family indicated that Jesse might not have been as diligent as she should in following her doctor's advice with regard to the high blood pressure, but they were not sure. This further complicated matters, said Dr Marrone. In a reassuring and hopeful tone Dr Marrone promised the family that everything possible would be done for Jesse, but he was clear in saying that she might die. He painted a picture for the family of serious injury, complicated by a pre-existing chronic health problem, with an as yet unknown outcome. There was a real chance of death, but it was not an inevitability. He simply could not say what the outcome would be. The family was visibly stunned, and said nothing after Dr Marrone had finished.

After talking with the Smith family, Dr Marrone left the conference room to meet the second family in the corridor outside the burn unit. The Stanford family was white and middle class, and some of them were visibly agitated. He began by summarizing the severity of patient Bill Stanford's condition. His injuries were very serious – burns over more than 60 per cent of his body including his face. (Jesse Smith was burned over 40 per cent of her body.) Marrone then told the family that the prognosis was best for younger people in good health, and that while Bill was in his early forties, Dr Marrone understood that Bill was indeed in good health. A family member quickly responded saying that yes, Bill was in good health and in good shape. He worked out regularly and ran, she added. Another family member interrupted to ask Marrone how Bill was doing relatively speaking – in terms of other people as severely burned. Her tone was sharp and her approach was aggressive. Marrone hesitated, and then responded somewhat evasively by saying that ten years ago someone in this condition would not survive; but advances in treatment such as newer topical medications to control infection mean that many such patients now did survive. He then tried to explain how burns are treated, but was interrupted again by the same person. She said that it was her understanding that recovery could take a long time, a matter of years. Dr Marrone answered that, yes, total recovery could take a long time, but he added that within seven months some people are able to function sufficiently to return to their jobs while recovery continues. He could not say what would happen in Bill's case.

Undaunted by Dr Marrone's avoidance of clear and certain answers, this family member then asked bluntly whether there was any reason for optimism – would Bill live? A resident with whom the family spoke the night of Bill's admission to the burn unit seemed pessimistic, she stated. This greatly upset the family. Could the family be hopeful, she asked, saying that she understood that if a burn patient survives the first two weeks then he would make it. Dr Marrone, still unwilling to provide answers with precise and certain benchmarks for this case, tried to avoid making any predictions about the outcome. He at first dismissed the two-week theory, but then agreed that the first *few weeks* (his emphasis) were crucial. He said that he had had patients in the burn unit who had done well for a number of weeks and then something suddenly and unexpectedly went wrong and the patient died. The family member, still searching for some benchmarks or a hint of predictability, then asked Marrone if the family could be more optimistic each day Bill survived. Yes, Marrone responded, and then he turned to the more basic issue underlying her aggressive line of questioning. Realistically, he could not say that Bill would not die. Bill's condition, Marrone said, was very serious, but he had suffered no pulmonary injury and was in good health at the time of the accident. Bill was stable and progressing; he tolerated the first surgery well. But Dr Marrone again emphatically stated he could not say that Bill would not die. Bill still had a long way to go.

These two examples illustrate that the idea of uncertainty can indeed be used to 'manage' families, especially more aggressive families like the Stanfords. The conference with the Stanford family also illustrates that for some people outside the medical world medicine is expected to be a much more exact and predictable science than it is for those inside. At first glance, it might appear that Dr Marrone was just being evasive, covering himself by 'hanging crepe' in case a patient should die – particularly in Bill Stanford's case, since he had been forewarned by the burn unit social worker during the unit's weekly meeting that the family might be a problem. In this way, he might be less likely to be held accountable, especially when confronted by a family that assumed that there was a fair amount of certainty in the treatment of burn victims and that Dr Marrone could give them answers accordingly.

There is another side to uncertainty in these two cases. Shortly after the two conferences, Dr Marrone discussed them with me. He emphasized the need to reassure families, while being realistic. The uncertainty, however, was a clinical reality for Marrone, and not just a way to avoid accountability to a potentially hostile lay world. The problem, he said, was that one just could not know what would happen with patients like Smith and Stanford: 'In these patients [referring to severely burned patients generally] during the first couple of weeks, unless there's a real "fuck-up" [a major error], it's basically a wash. There's just so many things involved. There are so many things that can go wrong.' Because of the unique characteristics of each injury and the history each patient brought, he said, one could not predict what would happen or why. The clinical reality of such uncertainty also manifested itself in the practice of the burn unit nurses consciously to detach themselves emotionally from patients like Smith and Stanford who were severely injured. The reason again, I was told, was that there were just so many things that could go wrong, and the detachment was a way of dealing with the stress caused by the unpredictability of these cases.

Bill Stanford did survive, but Jesse Smith did not, even though she survived the crucial first few weeks. Jesse's death some weeks later was a severe blow to the burn unit staff because it came long after it was thought she had passed the crisis period. In talking with Dr Marrone after Jesse's death, he told me that she represented one of those cases in which the patient survived the crisis period and was doing well – then suddenly died. Jesse died following respiratory arrest after being extubated (having the ventilator tube removed) following surgery the day before, which then triggered cardiac arrest (the respiratory arrest, he noted, was most likely tied to her inhalation injury, and the cardiac arrest to her pre-injury health problems). I asked Marrone if Jesse would have lived if she had been left on the ventilator to help her breathing, and he said that was unclear. He said: 'It's possible that she may have pulled through.' Bill Stanford, on the other hand, represents what Dr Marrone calls one of the unit's 'saves' – patients who would generally die but manage to pull through. Interestingly, even in retrospect Dr Marrone found it difficult to explain such a 'save' in a way that could be generalized or fully articulated.

These two cases illustrate one more facet of uncertainty for the medical workers I observed and its ultimate source in their view. When all is said and done, uncertainty has to do with the application of a general and imperfect body of knowledge to individual clinical cases. Perhaps the best characterization of the challenges for medical workers posed by uncertainty and contingency is found in Strauss *et al.* (1985: 19–20). They capture nicely the essence of the response when I asked GC people to articulate the matter. Strauss *et al.* drew the following analogy which they contrasted to precise, rational, scientific decision-making:

> Managing illness trajectories is more like the work of Mark Twain's celebrated Mississippi River pilot [than precise, rational, scientific decision-making]: the river was tricky, changed its course slightly from day to day, so even an experienced, but an inatten:.ve pilot could run into grave difficulties; worse yet, sometimes the river drastically shifted in its bed for some miles into quite a new course . . . The physician's and staff's management may be even more complex and the outcome of their work even more fateful than the pilot's. Some of the various contingencies may be anticipated, but only a portion of them may be relatively controllable, while some contingencies are quite unforeseeable, stemming as they do not only from the illnesses themselves but from organizational sources.
>
> (Strauss *et al.* 1985: 19–20)

Additionally, Strauss *et al.* note that the contingencies and uncertainties with which the medical pilots must deal stem not only from the limitations of medical science and personal skill, 'but also from a host of work and organizational sources as well as from biographical and lifestyle sources pertaining to patients, kin, and staff members themselves' (Strauss *et al.* 1985: 19).

This means there will always be some amount of randomness in the actual clinical practice of medicine. Indeed, Paget (1988) characterizes the clinical practice of medicine as being an inherently stochastic process. Each patient brings with him or her a unique medical history (Jesse Smith's hypertension), a unique social situation and personality (Bill Stanford's strong family network and his being a 'health nut' who worked-out often and wanted to keep himself in top shape), in addition to the particulars of the immediate medical problem (Jesse suffered an inhalation injury, while Bill did not). All these things can affect the course of medical treatment and its success in ways that are difficult to predict. Even in those areas in which medical science is more certain, there is still the question of what will happen when that relatively more certain knowledge is applied to a specific patient. This is what makes uncertainty inherent, because even if we were to assume that medical science – or some part of it – was to become certain and complete in its knowledge, uncertainty will always remain because of the variety of unique individuals to which it will be applied. In Paget's words:

> Clinical acts are especially unpredictable because they are forged in the uniquely constituted instance with uncertain and irregular knowledge. This does not mean that they are entirely unpredictable. Physicians work

with probabilities, for example, that certain illnesses are present in particular age groups or with probabilities that several diagnostic cues suggest a particular disease. The difficulty is that these probabilities do not predict the specific instance, and it is the specific instance that matters.

(Paget 1988: 46)

Ultimately, it is this uncertainty, dealt with by medical workers who are themselves all too human, that makes error inevitable.

Error is inevitable in medical work because of the very nature of medical work, and so the potential for error is pervasive. It is not a phenomenon that can be discretely defined and isolated from work in the context of a specific case. It is an inherent characteristic of medical work and cannot be eliminated. It can and must be managed, however, as the river pilot analogy implies. And this is always a part of the message the Chairman tries to convey with his burn unit anecdote about errors. Errors occur in 'the interplay between the efforts to control illness and contingencies', say Strauss *et al.* (1985: 19). Looked at in this way, one discovers that medical work is often consciously organized around the inevitability and pervasiveness of error and around the effort of managing uncertainty and contingency in order to minimize the potential for error.

In effect, then, the very organization of medical work is a reflection of the idea of error as an existential reality and central characteristic of medical work. This can be seen, for instance, in the very existence of specialized care units such as a surgical intensive care unit (ICU) or a burn unit. It can be seen in the creation of and reliance on detailed written 'protocols' laying out standardized ways for dealing with certain situations. The burn unit, for example, has a very detailed written protocol to follow when admitting a new patient to the unit. Standardizing things is intended to remove ambiguity and the occasion for individual decision and judgement, and a failure to follow the protocol is likely to be treated by superiors as a serious error in itself regardless of the patient outcome. A protocol error is, in effect, a violation of a set of normative standards, and such a violation threatens the entire scheme for managing error. The organization of work around the potential for error is also seen in the staffing of a unit to include specialists to handle particularly error-prone activities, rather than relying on the skills and knowledge of a generalist or non-specialist. For example, the burn unit and the surgical ICU each have an anaesthesia resident assigned in addition to the surgery residents because of their extensive use of powerful pain-killing drugs and need for specialized airway management.

Though largely invisible to the outside observer, and hardly mentioned in the literature, the efforts to manage contingency, uncertainty and error can be extensive. Such efforts again illustrate the centrality of uncertainty and error in medical work. Two very different examples show the range of these efforts. The first comes from the files of the physician who created GC's burn unit. He took the leading role in the design of what was to be *his* unit. One piece of correspondence in the file was his copy of a memo between two members of GC's administration working with this physician on the burn unit's planning and design. The memo dealt with comments of GC's General Services Department (janitorial, maintenance, etc.) on the plans for the unit. As might be expected, it discussed a variety of mundane matters, but its main concern was lessening the potential sources of infection. Minimizing the potential sources of infection is of utmost importance in any surgical ICU, but it is absolutely crucial in a burn unit given the already compromised condition of the patients. Infection is a major contingency and, while it cannot be eliminated, it can be minimized and controlled. Under the heading of 'Physical Characteristics' General Services had the following comments about things to consider in managing the problem of infection:

> Every effort should be made to use materials on walls, floors, and plumbing that would eliminate culture sites. Non-porous wall coverings: i.e., ceramic tile, and seamless flooring that can be easily washed and disinfected should be emphasized. Careful consideration must be given to the problem of chemical stains from silver nitrate, disinfectants, etc., in the choice of floor and wall materials. Efforts should be made to avoid the use of natural wood surfaces. Formica, stainless steel, ceramic tile, etc., are all washable with a wet, detergent germicidal solution without damage. Painted surfaces should be avoided whenever possible (including door frames) in favour of tile and plastics. This will circumvent the need for evacuation of the unit to restore painted surfaces or the problems incurred with painting without evacuation. Lighting fixtures in any unit of this type are a housekeeping problem – especially true in the case of a unit where low dust levels are critical. Installation of plumbing for clean and dirty purposes should be accomplished in such a manner as to make it both accessible and distinct. This was not done in S4 where the dirty sink was placed in an inaccessible area resulting in the clean sink being used for the discarding of urine at a handwashing site.

The second example is quite different, and comes from the efforts that were taking place at the time of this study to change the nature of the general surgical ICU and make it a specialized critical care unit. The present unit had long been a problem in terms of its management, and there had been a number of malpractice complaints. To deal with the problem the Chairman brought in a new head for the unit from the outside, who was given the task of straightening things out and upgrading the unit. More will be said on these efforts later.

For *every* step in the organization of medical work there is the potential for error. 'Mistakes are inevitable, or at least probable, made by someone, at some time during the carrying out of every single task. Alas, none are so simple, so easily done, as not to make error possible' (Strauss *et al.* 1985: 243–4). This is the working assumption behind the Chairman's story and behind much of the way in which medical work is organized. It is for this reason that so much attention is paid to managing uncertainty and contingency, and why processes and mechanisms develop for monitoring and handling error and for dealing with its consequences. When there is management failure, or little real management of error in practice, the consequences for the patient may be devastating or even fatal. It is the 'royal fuck-ups', as Dr Marrone colourfully says, that lead to trouble and malpractice claims. These events, he notes, seem to occur when management fails or is non-existent.

ORGANIZATION OF MEDICAL WORK

While the way in which medical work is organized is a response to uncertainty and a way of managing error, it is very much a mixed blessing. The dynamics surrounding the organization of medical work are themselves another source of uncertainty in the work environment as well as often being an impediment to the management of error. Two aspects of this process need to be explored with this in mind if we are to see how the organization of work reflects the meaning of error. The first are the dynamics created by the larger organizational context in which a given unit exists. The second involves the organization of work within the unit itself. The perception of problems at either level and the ways in which they are dealt with are a key part of what error means in practice.

The larger organizational context

Starting with the larger organizational context, work within hospitals is strictly divided among a number of specific units based on specialization. Strauss, *et al.* (1985: 5–6) suggest that 'a useful way of conceiving of the hospital is as a large number of work sites'. It consists 'of variegated workshops – places where different kinds of work are going on, where very different resources (space, skills, ratios of labour force, equipment, drugs, supplies, and the like) are required to carry out that work, where the divisions of labour are amazingly different, though all of this is in the direct or indirect service of managing patients' illnesses' (1985: 6). Much of a hospital's internal organization is based on a relatively strict division of labour which in turn is based on different sets of very specialized and non-interchangeable skills (i.e. radiology, surgery, pathology, etc.). Because of the nature of the skills involved – each skill devoted to significantly reducing uncertainty in a well-defined arena – each of these workshops is likely to have – or demand – a high degree of autonomy with expertise being the claim to authority.

Although the different units within the hospital, especially those involved in direct patient care and treatment, have a high degree of autonomy, none can operate as a totally independent entity. Each is dependent to some degree on the special expertise of other units in order to perform its functions. The burn unit, for example, relies heavily on the physical therapy department in the treatment of burn patients. More fundamentally, all patient care units are dependent on nursing administration for the assignment of a sufficient number of adequately skilled nurses. This means that medical work within a given unit, as well as the successful management of error, will be influenced by such dependencies. As a result, they create another level of uncertainty and contingency in addition to those caused by the limitations of medical science and personal skill. While an organizational structure based on expertise may help to reduce or control one kind of uncertainty, it creates another.[10] For the two units I observed at GC, this organizational dependence was indeed a major source of uncertainty and error.

The increasing specialization of medical work in response to uncertainty has made hospitals, especially major medical centres like GC, very complex organizations. The authors of one leading textbook on hospital management go so far as to say that 'the hospital is one of the most complex organizations in our society' (Schulz and Johnson 1983: 48). Viewed from the perspective of the insiders, a large hospital may seem to resemble what some organizational theorists call 'organized anarchy' rather than an entity comprising rational structures and relationships (March and Olsen 1976: 252): 'an organized anarchy is an organization typified by unclear goals, poorly understood technology, and variable participation'. With regard to the goals or functions of hospitals, that same textbook notes that 'while the function of the hospital may appear to be obvious, in reality hospitals have multiple functions that are not only changing over time, but are in some respects conflicting' (Schulz and Johnson, 1983: 53).

At GC, for instance, there could often be conflict among such major goals as patient care, teaching, research and financial solvency. We have already noted the uncertainty and limitations of medical science, but the situation is aggravated by organization based on specialization. As more and more workers concentrate on reducing uncertainty in their own area of specialization, there are likely to be fewer people with any in-depth understanding of other areas of specialization or any real sense of the whole, thus making most areas beyond one's own only marginally understood. And with regard to participation in organizational decision-making, the pattern for the people I observed was quite variable. People would, for the most part, invest time to the extent that a matter affected their work or unit. Otherwise, they felt they had more important things to do.

At GC, the result of such anarchy is that each unit operated in an ambiguous and often politically charged environment in which the protection of autonomy – of turf and status – was extremely important. While for a given unit relations with some units were cordial and co-operative, relations with other units were only marginally tolerable and the result of careful political negotiation. The relations with still other units, however, were downright hostile. The goals of different units clashed; their motivations and incentive structures differed. There was distrust and hostility because of differing approaches to treatment, because of turf battles over patients or resources, or simply because of a lack of understanding and communication. In addition, a unit's disagreements could be with the administration itself, and they involved conflicting goals and interests – especially in those situations in which the administration raised the issues of finances and staffing.

From the perspective of those working in the two units I observed at GC, their units operated within a very ambiguous and politically charged environment, both in terms of their respective relationships with other units (and each other!) and with the administration. The kinds of problem each unit faced varied from chronically late deliveries from the pharmacy to serious disagreements with the administration's new policy of staffing for nurses as a means of cost-containment to bitter feuds between services over the control of patients in an ICU. These problems, and similar ones, had a serious effect on each unit's ability to deal with the uncertainties caused by limitations of science and skill, thereby undermining their ability to manage error. For instance, there was an elaborate protocol system for dealing with severely burned patients for their first few weeks in the burn unit (the crucial first few weeks). It depended on at least two nurses being assigned to the patient around the clock (at least two-to-one nursing), and it would not work if nursing administration decided to save money by no longer allowing even one-to-one nursing. Additionally, some problems – like those with the pharmacy – were themselves seen as errors the unit had to handle.

An example from the general surgery ICU illustrates quite well the problematic nature of the organizational environment in which individual units operated. It comes from a conversation I had with the attending physician in charge of the surgical ICU, Dr Devlin, following a serious and near fatal error. The error involved a patient in the unit who was under the care of the surgical service that was the unit's heaviest user (and harshest critic) – the Very Best Service (VBS). The event occurred during a time when Dr Devlin was trying to gain more actual administrative and medical control over an essentially open unit.[11] (Devlin was the outside person brought in by the Chairman as part of his effort to upgrade this ICU.) Dr Devlin's goal was to make the general surgery ICU into a closed unit as a way of minimizing and handling error and so reduce disputes about the quality of care.

When asked about the consequences of the near fatal incident in the light of his goal, Dr Devlin said 'not good!'. He asked me what I knew about the political situation surrounding the unit and involving the surgical services using the unit. I indicated that I knew little about the politics, and he then proceeded to outline for me the predicament he faced in trying to exercise more control over the ICU. He said:

> Well, the politics are very serious and the political impact of this incident will not be good. This patient was on the Very Best Service, and they don't want anyone interfering with their patients. They think that no one but themselves should be involved with their patients and that there's nothing we can do or say that's helpful. So here we have a real 'screw-up' with one of their patients, and they'll use this incident as another example [that only they can handle their patients]. It will really set back our efforts to get this unit going. We want to upgrade this unit as a specialized critical care unit, and the VBS is fighting this because they don't think anyone else can care for their patients as well as they can.
>
> What's really bad is that there were two other incidents last week . . . [Question: Were they major problems?] . . . Yes, politically. One involved changing a ventilator setting for one of their patients to make the patient more comfortable. [Note: changed by one of the ICU residents] They weren't called and they were really mad when they found out. The other dealt with a suggestion noted in a chart [Note: by the same resident] about an apparent pneumothorax in one of their patients which they took as a criticism.

When asked if things with the VBS might improve when the rotation in the service changed, Dr Devlin's answer pointed to another factor aggravating the political situation – personalities. He said:

> things may get worse next month when Dr Bergels is on rotation. He's one of those people who will say whatever he thinks about someone and

what they do, and he'll write it in the chart. He's very abrasive and very protective of patients. He doesn't think there is much we can do for their patients in the unit. They know best, and these incidents may really set him off.

When asked if Dr Bergels or other VBS physicians would come to him to complain about such incidents and thereby give him a chance to explain things and help to lessen the political tensions, Dr Devlin's response was negative and graphic:

> No! You have to understand physicians. They indulge in passive–aggressive behaviour. The VBS people won't say anything directly to me. It will just fester. You know, white collar professionals are not like blue collar workers. When they [blue collar workers] have a problem at work, they just meet in the parking lot after work and settle it.
>
> [Question: Is there anything you can do to keep Dr Bergels from causing too many problems for the unit?] . . . Not really. There's not much I can do. If he gets really bad, I can shut him out of the unit – not take in any of his patients. But that's too drastic. Politically, I can't do it. All I can do is tell him that I, or my service, won't refer any more patients to him.

Underlying this political conflict between Dr Devlin and the VBS, of course, were alternative and mutually exclusive judgements on how best to care for patients in the surgical ICU, and each was based on expertise. This is the irony built into the organization of medical work based on expertise as a means of managing the potential for error.

Work inside the unit

The organization of work within a unit itself causes its own uncertainties and potential for error, even though work is organized in a way to manage uncertainty and error better. Most of this work, of course, is not performed by physicians – or at least not attending physicians. Most day-to-day medical work is performed by other medical workers, following a relatively strict division of labour based on specialized training of one kind or another. Most medical work is performed by residents, students, nurses, aides, physical therapists, nutritionists and other specialized workers. They have the most frequent contact with patients, and so the greatest opportunity for error. Ironically, it is the use of such specialized or semi-specialized workers that is to help minimize uncertainty and hence error. This can be successful only if the physician in charge can meet the challenge of managing that additional potential for error by the way work in the unit is organized and controlled. Dr Devlin's efforts to upgrade the surgical ICU were an attempt to manage better that potential by co-ordinating patient care under the control of a specialized critical care staff.

This type of control already existed in the burn unit and is best illustrated by the unit's weekly interdisciplinary burn conference. The meeting is chaired by the attending physician in charge of the burn unit, and during the meeting each patient's chart is opened and the work and events of the past week are discussed along with the plans for the forthcoming week. Each discipline regularly involved in the care and treatment of burn patients is represented at this meeting: senior plastic surgery resident, burn service surgical residents, an anaesthesia resident, nurses, physical therapists, social workers (one for adults and another for children), microbiologists (who do much of the regular lab work for the unit), nutritionists, chaplains and discharge planning (to co-ordinate out-patient treatment after leaving the hospital). Special needs of particular patients may temporarily add to the participants – such as a psychiatrist or a paediatrician. At the time of this study the unit's director was negotiating for the addition of a psychiatry resident to the staff. The work of each of the different disciplines brings uncertainty and the potential for error that must be managed. This weekly interdisciplinary meeting is one of the major means by which the quality of work is regularly monitored and co-ordinated.

Understanding how organizational uncertainty within the unit itself is handled requires some understanding of how the work is structured and how the work of different health care professionals meshes. The work of different medical workers is seen as taking place at different levels which reflect differences in specialization as well as status differences within a well-understood hierarchy. Strauss *et al.* note three levels: planning and designing the course of treatment; implementing and supervising the tasks that go along with that plan; and the actual performance of those tasks. When talking about specialized units like ICUs which must operate within an ambiguous organizational context, two more levels of work can be added, both of which are not only key parts of the management of error but also potential sources of uncertainty and error in themselves. The fourth level involves what might be called external affairs and diplomacy – handling the politics of the unit's relations with other parts of the hospital. The fifth involves the design or vision and ongoing management of the unit itself – in short, leadership.

The first level of work – designing and planning the course of treatment – is the domain of attending physicians, and they normally have a great amount of freedom in handling their patients. This freedom is jealously guarded by most individuals, but can be a constant problem for an ICU and its staff as Dr Devlin's problems show. The second level of work is primarily the responsibility of the more senior residents to whom the attending physicians delegate a great deal of the day-to-day responsibility (their lieutenants, so to speak), and the nurses in a unit with administrative responsibilities. These two sets of people are responsible for seeing that the attending physician's orders are carried out by the appropriate worker. There is the potential of conflict, of course, if the attending physician's orders are not consistent with a unit's protocols and policies. The senior residents and nurses are also responsible for the smooth and orderly operation of the unit on a daily basis. In reality, most of the purely administrative and supervisory work falls on the nurses and is heavily dependent on detailed, written protocols and policies (where they exist *and* can be enforced).

The third level of work involves a much broader range of workers – those who actually perform the various tasks involved in the attending physician's plan for care and treatment. It involves nurses, residents, social workers, physical therapists, and so on; and this is the level at which most medical work (and error) takes place. Much of the work at this level is (or should be) controlled by written protocols and policies in a unit. By laying out – sometimes in minute detail – what is to be done in a given situation, these written protocols and policies are intended to reduce the amount of uncertainty for this level of work by routinizing tasks in accordance with the *unit's* approach to things. By reducing the need for judgement or guesswork at this level, the hope is to minimize opportunities for error. Much of the second level of work involves implementing and enforcing the unit's protocols and policies, and breaches of protocol and policy are considered serious errors since they not only endanger patients, but also pose a threat to the unit itself.

The fourth and fifth levels of work are of a different order, and are the sole province of the physician who directs the unit. The fourth level of work involves external affairs. More senior residents or nurses will handle some lower level, day-to-day matters with other parts of the hospital such as the informal negotiations to obtain a piece of equipment, or register a complaint with pharmacy over a problem with medication deliveries. Matters of any importance involving external affairs, however, are handled at the director's level because only he or she has the political capital to do anything. As the earlier example involving Dr Devlin shows, this level of work can be difficult and politically charged. The most important aspects of the director's handling of external affairs involve protecting and maintaining the unit's resources (both financial and personnel) and gaining and maintaining autonomy. Without autonomy and sufficient resources, a unit will not be able to manage uncertainty and error successfully.

The issue of autonomy, in turn, is related to the fifth level of work –

providing and maintaining a coherent vision of the unit and its purpose along with the ongoing management of the unit within the context of that vision. Without this vision no specialized unit is likely to work effectively and it is likely to have severe problems dealing with uncertainty and contingency. It is this vision, for instance, that will determine the substance of unit protocols and policies – its way of doing things. The director's vision provides the unit's mission and identity, and will include a particular philosophy of care and treatment. Because of the limitations in scientific knowledge, there can be severe disagreement over what that vision should be. Each vision represents a particular philosophy of managing uncertainty and error. For instance, at least one of Dr Marrone's senior colleagues had a very different idea of what the burn unit's vision should look like and regularly said so. What is important, from the perspective of uncertainty, is the institutionalization of *a* vision, rather than the particular vision ultimately chosen.

This vision is not only important internally, it also sends a message to the rest of the hospital about the unit's mission and philosophy. It tells outsiders what to expect. The importance of vision, and the political problems inherent in institutionalizing one, is illustrated by Dr Devlin's goal of upgrading the surgical ICU into a closed, specialized critical care unit under the director's control. Such an upgrade – putting into effect a particular vision – was seen as the answer to the problems of a unit beset by too much error and too many complaints about malpractice. Dr Devlin's problems in institutionalizing this vision were largely political since the vision means a net increase in autonomy for the unit and a net decrease for the surgical services using the unit (some of which wielded considerable political power in their own right).

The practical importance of these two levels of work – autonomy and vision – for the management of uncertainty and contingency can be seen in a comparison between the surgical ICU and the burn unit. In the former, a political struggle was under way to institutionalize a particular vision – a struggle with no guarantee of success. In the latter, a particular vision has been institutionalized for some time. To illustrate the difference, we can compare Dr Devlin's problems with the VBS to an incident in the burn unit regarding the transfer of a patient from another part of GC into that unit.

The patient was not a burn victim, but someone who had begun to develop severe and growing skin lesions all over her body. She had been in the medical centre's children's section and the staff there were unable to handle this patient's problems involving large, open areas on the body. One possible way of dealing with these problems was to transfer the patient to the burn unit because the staff there were equipped for and experienced in handling large, open skin wounds. Indeed, the goal of developing such an expertise was a part of the original vision behind the creation of a special-ized burn unit. A bed was open in the unit, but there was apparently some disagreement over who would direct the patient's care if she were moved to the burn unit – the current attending physician in the children's section or the director of the burn unit.

The ongoing negotiations on this transfer interrupted one of the weekly interdisciplinary burn conferences. A senior resident and a student came into the meeting and walked to the head of the conference table where Dr Marrone was sitting. They held a short, whispered conversation with him and then left. About ten minutes later they returned and began another whispered conversation with the director. In responding, Marrone this time spoke out loud for all in the meeting to hear.

> You tell Dr Riggins that there's a bed available and we can handle her if he wants. But if he's going to put her in this unit, I'm in charge, not him! I'll be more than happy to discuss things with him and consult him on treatment, but all major decisions are mine – I am in control completely. If he doesn't like it, he doesn't have to put her in here and that's it! There's no negotiation on that. That's the way it goes.

Dr Riggins apparently relented because later that day the patient was transferred to the burn unit with Dr Marrone in charge of her care.

Underlying what may appear on the surface to be a bold act of personal arrogance on Marrone's part was in reality a defence of the unit, its mission and its way of doing things – including its ways of dealing with uncertainty and managing error. Such a strong stand sent a clear message to those outside the unit, and expressing it out loud in a unit meeting also sent a clear message to those working in the unit, reinforcing the unit's sense of mission and its institutional integrity.

LABELLING ERRORS

While the nature of medical work makes it impossible for medical workers to articulate a precise, substantive definition of error that can be generally applied, the issue of how they know it when they see it remains. For the GC people I observed, an 'error' in any specific situation is likely to be identified and labelled as such only in retrospect, meaning that the worker involved may not know at the time that his or her actions or decisions constituted an error. Indeed, in some situations – because of the uncertainty – the worker cannot know in advance what would constitute an error. This is something that can be determined only in retrospect, after something has been done and as its consequences become evident. In the extreme, as Dr Marrone would frequently say, the only thing you know for sure is that if you do nothing the patient will die – and that's an error! In these situations, what becomes important is the process one follows in deciding what to do and then doing it (i.e. were the proper examinations done, were the proper tests used?, etc.). This means, as Bosk (1979: 24) notes, that error can be an essentially contested concept in practice.

Not all aspects of medical work present such a problematic situation with regard to labelling error. As one moves down the status hierarchy, from attending physician to the para-professionals and aides handling most of the innumerable mundane tasks comprising day-to-day work involving patients, things become less contested and the boundaries of proper action clearer (see Jamous and Peloille 1970). This is because work becomes more routinized and governed by set protocols and policies that can and should be known in advance. Deviations from appropriate and expected performance are more identifiable as we go down the status hierarchy. The retrospective process of examining events is still evident, but with clearer standards. Of course, it begs the question of whether the protocols and policies to which workers are expected to adhere are the most appropriate and beneficial to the patients – something that will always be debatable.

Most errors – regardless of what or who they involve – become errors as a result of a retrospective problem-solving process of sorts. Errors are socially constructed. Few events are immediately obvious as being an error and recognized as such within the unit. It is only after some untoward event occurs to a patient – or a patient dies – that the most exacting scrutiny will be applied, including the invocation of formal peer review or disciplinary mechanisms. There is no guarantee, however, that such probing scrutiny will always be the rule. Only after something triggers a question about a patient's condition or a worker's conduct does the social process begin that may lead to an event being labelled an error. Short of a patient's death or some obvious change in condition, questionable events may be identified through some regular monitoring device (like rounds or the weekly burn conference) or through some irregular or chance review of a patient or his or her chart. It is quite possible, however, that events that may well be labelled as errors if discovered are simply not noticed.

This labelling process is characterized by talk on the part of the workers in a unit. Since there are no clear standards to apply, like a template or checklist, in any except the most mundane situations problematic events are explored, reconstructed and discussed over some period through formal mechanisms such as mortality and morbidity conferences, and more important through informal discussions and discussion among the various workers involved in the case. Paget has pointed out that talking about problematic medical events is very important. Talk 'examines and inquires in order to discover what went wrong . . . Talk also attempts to preserve the possibilities of action, some viable place from which to act again in an error-ridden activity' (Paget 1988: 89). In addition, the talking is a part of the effort given to building as much consensus as possible on the labelling of an event as an error. Building a consensus is very important in maintaining the integrity of the unit's mission and its ways of managing uncertainty and error. For some things, like the violation of a protocol, this task is relatively easy. For other things, like the decision on how aggressively to treat a patient with burns over more than 90 per cent of the body, the issues are so difficult that no consensus will emerge.

Even in the least problematic situations, such as a protocol error on the part of a nurse or a para-professional, this social process does not end with the attachment of the label. Some effort must be made to defend and justify the label and this involves not only a reconstruction of what happened but also an interpretation and evaluation of the event. Why did things happen as they appear to have? This question can render the most unproblematic situations – a protocol error – problematical. The question of why things happened as they did is closely tied to the issue of blame and fault. This question is of the utmost practical importance. The assignment of blame and fault will determine what remedial measures will be taken, if any.

Errors committed by and blamed on an individual worker are likely to lead only to the disciplining of that worker, and the action can run from a 'private talk' (reading someone the 'riot act'), to a public admonition (in a meeting or on rounds), to the invocation of a formal disciplinary process (putting a nurse on report), to the extreme sanction of dismissal. A repeated error (repeated by different workers over some period of time) may lead to a protocol or policy adjustment to ensure better quality and will almost certainly lead to an 'in service' (such as a presentation by physical therapy on the proper use of splints after a number of weeks of errors in putting on splints in the burn unit) and mini-lectures in weekly conferences (such as the causes and prevention of ear problems with bed-ridden patients). An isolated error committed by an individual, where no blame or fault is assigned, is unlikely to lead to any real response. Still, the talk surrounding such an event and its retrospective evaluation will help to ensure that the event serves as a learning experience both for the individual worker and for others. Again, medicine is an inexact science. The death of Jesse Smith, discussed earlier, provides an example of error without blame as well as the retrospective labelling process.

This case received very close scrutiny because Jesse's death was so unexpected. Dr Marrone investigated this matter himself – reviewing the chart and talking with each of the nurses and residents involved in her care in the unit. The case was presented and discussed at the appropriate mortality and morbidity conference as well as at the weekly burn conference. It was a constant topic of conversation for nearly two weeks and during this time it was also discussed at burn unit rounds and the surgical service's rounds.

The key event in Marrone's reconstruction of events was the resident's decision to remove Jesse from the ventilator following surgery. In Marrone's judgement, Jesse would not have died if she had remained on the ventilator and this meant that the resident's decision was an error – but an error in retrospect. Paget also emphasizes the time structure of errors which she captures in the following quotation from a physician she interviewed: 'the errors are errors now, but weren't errors then' (1988: 36). The resident treating Jesse could not have known at that time that her decision was an error, Marrone said. She had examined the patient thoroughly; had all the appropriate tests done and readings made; and all the results were well within the parameters to remove a patient with Jesse's history and injury from the ventilator. The resident had done everything that should have been done and she made an appropriate decision. The only problem was that the patient died. This was, Marrone said, a 'forgivable' or 'excusable' error. In other words, no blame or fault was assigned to the resident. This was, in his estimation, one of those situations in which medical work's uncertainties and contingencies prevailed. If the resident had not personally examined the patient herself and had all the appropriate tests done, blame would have been assigned to the resident.

It is possible for the retrospective construction and labelling of error to pinpoint a particular medical worker as the one who has committed error, but to assign blame to another person or an entity elsewhere in the hospital. This again exonerates the worker in the unit while upholding the unit's approach to managing uncertainty and error. Towards the end of my field-work, there was an increasing problem with errors by nurses in both the burn unit and the surgical ICU that provides an illustration of such blame shifting. Protocols and policies were not always followed as diligently as required by some of the nurses, and many daily nursing tasks were left undone, only partially done or done late. As these situations were evaluated through regular meetings (i.e. the weekly burn conference) and through informal investigation, the blame was ultimately assigned to nursing administration and its new staffing policies, thereby exonerating the unit nurses. These policies cut back on the number of nurses assigned to ICUs (i.e. such as no one-to-one nursing despite unit policies requiring it) in the name of cost-containment. The practical consequence of these new staffing policies was an *ad hoc* reallocation of effort by the nurses working in each unit to give the most sick patients the intensive nursing care called for at the expense of the less sick and at the expense of administrative duties. Things became so bad in the surgical ICU that one nurse, in exasperation, remarked at the end of a twelve-hour shift (plus two hours of overtime), during which the surgical ICU was operating with a reduced nursing staff, that she was just relieved they had got through the night without killing a patient. Nursing morale dropped significantly, further increasing the potential for error. The shift in blame from the nurses themselves to nursing administration came as more and more events were labelled as errors and as nursing morale dropped even more in response. Some of the nurses began complaining of being placed between 'a rock and a hard place' – yes, there were errors but there was no way to remedy things. In the burn unit, some senior nurses were even talking of leaving. The key factor in causing the shift in blame seems to have been an edict by nursing administration that any nurses who complained to the unit director about the negative effects of the new staffing policies would be fired.

Once the blame was assigned to nursing administration by the unit directors, nurses were effectively exonerated. The efforts to deal with the problem switched from attempting to discipline individual nurses to bringing political pressure to bear on nursing administration to abandon its new staffing policies. These efforts included having the critical care committee – the major quality assurance body for ICUs – devise standards for staffing in the name of quality assurance. The legal affairs office was also involved in this effort by virtue of the argument that the consequences of the staffing policies put the hospital at serious risk of malpractice claims. When my fieldwork ended, this political battle was still under way.

A less dramatic and more typical example of shifting blame involved a medication for a burn unit patient. The medication was to be given at a particular time during the night nursing shift. When the burn unit resident arrived first thing in the morning and began casually looking over the charts, he noticed that the ordered medication had not been given. He became angry and checked to see which nurse was caring for this patient. He discovered that she had left as soon as her shift ended. Not administering this medication was, in his view, a serious error on the nurse's part given the patient's situation, one for which she most likely would have to take the blame and face disciplinary action. He wanted to place her on report. The incident was reported to Dr Marrone who concurred with the resident on the seriousness of the error in this case. He was not as quick to make a judgement on blame.

Dr Marrone instructed a senior nurse, who served as the burn unit co-ordinator, to find out why the error occurred since it involved a nurse with a good reputation. After talking with the nurse involved, the other nurses on duty and the resident on call that night, the senior nurse was able to piece together an explanation. The nurse had called the pharmacy earlier in that shift to order the required medication (individual units no longer kept many medications in their stores since centralizing things in the pharmacy was seen by the administration as being more cost efficient). When the order did not arrive as scheduled, the nurse called the pharmacy again. Pharmacy said they were shorthanded and too busy to deliver it at that time. Because of her duties, the nurse could not leave the unit to get the medication. Instead she called her nursing supervisor who in turn called the pharmacy, again with no success. The nurse then phoned the surgical resident on call, once again with no success; and the pharmacy never did deliver the medication that night. This reconstruction of events was discussed at the weekly burn conference one week after the event (the event had occurred the night before the previous week's conference and much of that discussion was driven by the resident's anger and desire for immediate disciplinary action against the nurse). The nurse was not put on report, and the blame was placed on the pharmacy, which was an easy target given an ongoing set of problems with that department. Instead of disciplining the nurse, discussion at the burn conference centred on adjustments in unit practices and policies to deal with a similar problem in the future. These included telephoning Dr Marrone or another attending physician right away – rather than going through the on-call chain that eventually leads to the director – as well as exploring the possibility of keeping larger amounts of regularly used medications on hand in the unit. Dr Marrone also indicated that he would contact his counterpart in the pharmacy to discuss the incident.

This labelling process appears to categorize errors in two ways in addition to the assignment of blame. It categorizes errors into a number of substantive categories – such as judgement errors, technical errors, machine errors, protocol errors, management or administrative errors, diplomacy errors, and so on. It also categorizes errors on the basis of their handling and threat to the unit *once* identified and labelled. There are four broad types: potentially catastrophic errors; serious but not catastrophic errors; routine errors; and minor transgressions.

Potentially catastrophic errors are those perceived to threaten the unit itself, and they involve higher levels of authority within the hospital in their handling. These are situations seen as not manageable on the unit level. A unit director, for example, may take the issue immediately to the legal affairs office or it may be taken to a major peer review or policy-making/quality assurance committee within the hospital or to the medical ethics committee.

An example from the burn unit involved a task error by a nurse caring for a child. She did not adequately monitor the IV lines on the child and a problem resulted that required immediate, but not major, remedial surgery. The problem was one that could easily have been prevented if the nurse had been more vigilant in monitoring the patient. The child's mother, already very upset because of the child's burn injuries and the possibility of disfigurement, became enraged and stated that she was going to sue the hospital if any harm came to her child. Based on their assessment of the mother and her intentions, the nurses immediately called Dr Marrone. He, in turn, brought in the legal affairs office to mediate in the light of the mother's threat (which was taken seriously). Another example, of a different sort, can be found in the way in which the new nursing policies discussed earlier were being handled – taking the issue to the critical care committee (the major policy-making/quality assurance committee for ICUs) and involving legal affairs in the battle.

Below catastrophic errors are a class of problems serious enough to warrant attention beyond the unit, but not serious enough to warrant crisis management. These situations are not seen as threatening the unit itself, although they can cause substantial problems for the person responsible. These situations will rise to the service or departmental level for handling through existing review mechanisms such as general rounds or mortality and morbidity conferences. The death of patient Jesse Smith reached this level, but the situation was not seen as serious enough to warrant crisis management.

Routine errors are those handled within the unit itself through its own ongoing mechanisms. In the burn unit, for example, the weekly burn conference acts as an important monitoring device for smaller errors involving routinized work and their handling. The typical review of a patient's treatment over the previous week may point out some untoward event or lapse from expected performance in the light of existing protocols and policies. Such issues are usually discussed and the responsible worker or workers are chastised. If needed, some remedy is suggested to prevent a reoccurrence. Typical of such errors were protocol or policy errors resulting from the regular rotations of various types of worker in the unit (i.e. residents, physical therapists, etc.) or the turnover of nurses or the use of 'rent-a-nurses'. Each new worker must learn the unit's written and unwritten rules and requirements, and the learning process often comes through making mistakes which are later discussed at the weekly conference.

Finally, there are the innumerable minor transgressions which never reach the attention of mechanisms like the weekly burn conference. These may include missing a chart entry, misfiling an X-ray, neglecting to fill out a meal report for calorie intake, and the like. Typically, these errors involve record-keeping and clerical tasks, and they are dealt with informally by a more senior resident or more senior nurse talking to the worker responsible. Sometimes, not even this happens because the transgression is discovered and corrected by someone else with little concern over the error's origin (we all make little mistakes or forget bureaucratic matters once in a while).

Although this rough scale of errors reflects harm to the patient, it is not a necessary correlation. The key to the rough measurement standard is the threat to the unit or service (and often attending physician) in control of the patient or the threat to the hospital itself. While something related to a patient's death is never treated as a minor transgression, not everything treated as serious or catastrophic involves fatality. In fact, things treated as serious or even catastrophic may involve easily remedied mistakes, but very aggressive patients or families. More than anything, it is the perceived threat that is important. What is ultimately at stake is organizational viability – the survival of the unit or service, or at least survival as constituted at present (recall the perceived need to change the character of surgical ICU discussed earlier). The burn unit, for instance, had been a perennial big money loser for GC and so there was constant pressure from the hospital administration to keep its loss experience within a set range or face the prospect of being closed. One or two large malpractice claims could make the difference, as could a wrong decision (a judgement error) on trying to 'salvage' or not transfer a non-paying patient whose stay in the unit would extend for months. In fact, the story that always arose in conversations surrounding the fiscal state of the burn unit was the decision to try to save a non-paying patient who stayed in the unit for over five months at a cost of nearly $500,000 – a patient who never regained consciousness and eventually died.

CONCLUSION

To return to the point of the Chairman's burn unit story, error is seen as inevitable and even frequent. It is the result of the contingencies and uncertainties of what is believed to be an inexact science; of the unique characteristics and histories of individual patients; and of the organizational context in which medical work takes place. Error – or at least the potential for error – is pervasive, an artifact of medical work generally rather than just the work of physicians. Although error is pervasive, it cannot be defined in a way that is generally applicable. Instead, there is a retrospective labelling process that determines what constitutes an error in a particular, concrete situation. Two products of this process are likely to determine the response to an event labelled as an error: the assessment of blame and the perception of threat to the unit itself. The assessment of blame determines what will happen to the worker or workers involved and what may need to be done within the unit to rectify the problem. In short, the assessment of blame determines the remedial responses to an error. The level of threat to the unit determines whether actors outside the unit need to be involved in the management of an error, and especially whether some form of crisis management is needed.

From this perspective, formal disputes over medical care arise when appropriate mechanisms and processes for managing uncertainty and error do not exist or do not work sufficiently. This suggests that formal disputes are seen as failures of management rather than as failures of medical work *per se*. After all, there will always be failures in medical work, even blameworthy ones. The important thing is managing the inevitable. Issues of quality and accountability take on a whole new hue when seen in this light as do the efforts to manage uncertainty and error. Ideas of quality may be influenced by a host of factors that are important within a particular organizational context but have little to do with medical care *per se* (i.e. issues of cost-containment), and the layers of organization may so blur the idea of accountability that it becomes meaningless in any practical sense. Indeed, it is possible that uncertainty and error can be managed all too well with few formal disputes over the quality of care, while the actual quality from the patient's perspective is mediocre or worse. This, however, is not likely to happen because of the dynamics of organized anarchy. Greater organizational complexity and specialization as a means to manage uncertainty and error better may simply generate the potential for more disputes in the face of organized anarchy, and this threat may ultimately work to help maintain a higher level of quality for patient care.

NOTES

This research was supported in part by grants from the Fund for Research on Dispute Resolution and from the Robert Wood Johnson Foundation. The opinions expressed are the author's and do not necessarily reflect the position of the grantors or the American Bar Foundation. I would like to acknowledge the assistance of Dr Rubeena Mian, who participated in the fieldwork and handled innumerable technical matters. I would also like to thank Robert Dingwall, Leah Feldman, Bryant Garth, Joanne Martin, Susan Shapiro and Greg Stuart for their comments on earlier drafts of this chapter.

1 GC is a pseudonym, as are all the names used in this chapter.
2 Best estimates suggest that only a very small percentage of medical errors ultimately lead to medical malpractice litigation; see Daniels and Andrews 1989: 164–7; Danzon 1985: 20–5.
3 According to Strauss *et al.* (1985: 242): '*Analytic consideration of mistakes begins with central activity itself* (whether that is caring for patients, constructing building, or manufacturing automobiles). What is its nature and what are its salient properties? What are the arcs of work – with associated kinds and levels of tasks – entailed in the activity? The central activity provides the context and conditions for probable mistakes, their types, when they appear, where they appear, who will make them, the degree of difficulty in rectifying them, the types of consequences of mistakes made or rectified; also what risks are balanced against consideration of various types of potential errors and their estimated consequences.' (Emphasis in original.)

4 This meant focusing on rounds (both weekly service rounds and daily chart rounds in a unit); mortality and morbidity meetings (including closed meetings); unit staff meetings; nurses' reports at the end of shifts; monthly nurses' meetings in a unit; and the like.

5 See Strauss *et al.* (1985).

6 Freidson argues that because physicians must often exercise their judgement (which he says is synonymous with 'opinion'), it is easy to assume that there is no stable criterion for decision meaning that 'within general limits of known alternatives, every decision is equally correct at the time it is made' (Freidson 1975: 135). Consequently, he says, only the grossest mistakes would bring any scrutiny; but, he also argues, such mistakes rarely occur. 'With the rules removed, the criteria for evaluating one's own and one's colleagues' work become so permissive as to allow extremely wide variation in performance. Only gross or blatant acts of ignorance and inattention which all physicians would be united in recognizing and condemning remained securely in the category of deviant mistakes [as opposed to normal mistakes], but they were unlikely to be performed by any normal physician with an average medical education. Most of what remained beyond that seemed to be normalized. These events remained mistakes or errors, they were deviations from normal work expectations, but they did not call for reproach' (Freidson 1975: 137). In practice, he believes that this effectively isolates physicians from any accountability to the lay world. A similar approach and conclusion are found in Marcia Millman's study of the 'backrooms' of medicine (1977).

7 One can come away from Millman's discussion with the distinct impression that there is bad faith on the part of doctors with regard to the handling of errors. From such a perspective, the idea of uncertainty and the inevitability of error becomes but one more mechanism used in an ongoing pattern of fraud and misrepresentation perpetrated by doctors to protect themselves from the lay world.

8 In Bosk's view: 'It is further assumed that 'error . . . belongs to a class of events with such readily identifiable characteristics that on any occasion its recognition is deemed unproblematic. An event possesses the requisite characteristics and fits the class or it does not. Moreover, these attributes are specified in advance of the fact and not determined in a retrospective or *ex post facto* fashion . . . . Now, this categorical view of error displays both a misapprehension of the nature of medical decision-making and of the interactional dynamics which surround social control in a profession' (1979: 23).

9 For a discussion of such reactions to the questioning of understood, implicit values see Garfinkel 1967: 35–75.

10 In his history of the American hospital system, Rosenberg (1987: 4) notes that: 'Like the ship of fools that symbolized man's ineradicable frailties in early modern Europe, the hospital can be seen as a later twentieth-century symbol of the gap between human aspirations and necessary human failings.'

11 An open unit is one in which control over the care and treatment of patients in the unit remains in the hands of the admitting physician and his or her service rather than with the physicians staffing the ICU. A closed ICU (the burn unit is such a closed unit) is one in which a specialized staff has control of the care and treatment of patients in the unit. Once a patient leaves the unit, control reverts to the admitting physician. For a brief overview of the issues involved in the debate over closed versus open units, see Schenk 1988.

Bibliography

Action for Victims of Medical Accidents (1988) *Lawyers Service Newsletter*, March.

Adam, S. (1987) 'Creating a Quality Health Service: The Community Medicine Perspective', in *Creating Quality in the NHS*, Centre for Professional Development, Department of Community Medicine, The Medical School, Manchester.

Addiss, P. (1980) 'The Life History Complaint Case of Martha and George Rose; "Honouring the Warranty"', in Nader, L. (ed.), *No Access to Law: Alternatives to the American Judicial System*, New York: Academic Press.

Andreasen, A. (1975) *The Disadvantaged Consumer*, New York: Free Press.

Allsop, J. and May, A. (1986) *The Emperor's New Clothes: Family Practitioner Committees in the 1980s*, London: King's Fund.

Anrys, H. (1988) *Le Contexte Juridique de L'Evaluation des Soins Médicaux*, unpublished mimeo.

Arluke, A. (1977) 'Social Control Rituals in Medicine', in Dingwall, R., Heath, C., Reid, M. and Stacey, M. (eds), *Health Care and Health Knowledge*, London: Croom Helm.

Association of Community Health Councils for England and Wales (1990) *National Health Service Complaints Procedures*, London: ACHCEW.

Berwick, D. (1989) 'Continuous Improvement as an Ideal in Health Care', *New England Journal of Medicine* 320: 53–6.

Beske, F. (1989) *Results of Quality Assurance in the Federal Republic of Germany*, unpublished mimeo.

Beske, F., Brecht, J. and Niemann, F-M. (1989) *Qualitätssicherung in Krankenhäusern in Schleswig-Holstein: Grundsätze und Durchführungskonzept*, unpublished mimeo.

Beske, F., Niemann, F-M. and Horn, G-T. (1988) *Qualitätssicherung im Krankenhaus in der Bundesrepublik Deutschland*, Kiel: Gesundheits-System-Forschung.

Best, A. (1981) *When Consumers Complain*, New York: Columbia University Press.

Best, A. and Andreasen, A. (1976) *Talking Back to Business: Voiced and Unvoiced Consumer Complaints*, Washington Centre for the Study of Responsive Law, Call for Action Working Paper.

Black, D. (1976) *The Behavior of Law*, New York: Academic Press.

Black, D.J. (1973) 'The Mobilization of Law', *Journal of Legal Studies* 2: 125–49.

Black, N. (1990) 'Quality Assurance of Medical Care', *Journal of Public Health Medicine* 12: 97-104.

Blanpain, J.E. (1985) 'The Role of Medical Associations in Quality Assurance', *Health Policy* 4: 291–305.

Bosk, C. (1979) *Forgive and Remember: Managing Medical Failure*, Chicago: University of Chicago Press.

Boston, J. (1987) 'Transforming New Zealand's Public Sector: Labour's Quest for Improved Efficiency and Accountability', *Public Administration* 65: 423–42.

British Medical Association (1989) *Special Report on the Government's White Paper*, London: British Medical Association.

Brooks, T. (1989) 'Giving Accreditation Where It's Due', *Health Service Journal* March: 264–5.

Buck, N., Devlin, H. and Lunn, J. (1988), *The Report of a Confidential Enquiry into Perioperative Deaths*, London: Nuffield Provincial Hospitals Trust/King's Fund.

Buekens, P., Derom, R., Thiery, M., Bekaert, A. and Vlietinck, R. (1987) 'Quality Assurance of Obstetrical Care in Belgium', *Australian Clinical Review* June: 69–72.

Bundesärztekammer (1989) *Tätigkeitsberichit*, Köln-Lovenich: Deutscher Ärzte-Verlag.

Bundesrat (1988) 'Entwurf eines Gestetzes zur Strukturreform im Gesundheitswesen', *Gesetzentwurf der Bundesregierung*, 29 April.

'Called to Account' (1989) *The Lancet* i: 545–6, 605–6, 661–2, 714–16.

Crombie, D. and Fleming, D. (1988) *Practice Activity Analysis*, London: Royal College of General Practitioners.

Daniels, S. and Andrews, L. (1989) 'The Shadow of the Law: Jury Decisions in Obstetrics and Gynecology Cases', in Rostow, V. and Bulger, R. (eds), *Medical Professional Liability and the Delivery of Obstetrical Care*, Washington, DC: National Academy Press.

Daniels, S. and Martin, J. (1990) 'Myth and Reality in Punitive Damages', *Minnesota Law Review* 75: 1–64.

Danzon, P. (1985) *Medical Malpractice: Theory, Evidence, and Public Policy*, Cambridge, Mass: Harvard University Press.

Davis, F. (1960) 'Uncertainty in Medical Prognosis: Clinical and Functional', *American Journal of Sociology* 66: 41–7.

Deal, T.E. and Kennedy, A.A. (1982) *Corporate Cultures*. Reading, Mass: Addison-Wesley.

Department of Health (1988) *Health and Personal Social Services Statistics*, London: HMSO.

Department of Health (1989a) *Working for Patients*, Cmd. 555, London: HMSO.

Department of Health (1989b) *Working for Patients: Working Paper 6: Medical Audit*, London: HMSO.

Department of Health (1989c) *Report on Confidential Enquiries into Maternal Deaths in England and Wales, 1982–84*, London: HMSO.

Department of Health (1989d) *Working Paper 1: Self-Governing Hospitals*, London: HMSO.

Department of Health (1989e) *Working Paper 4: Indicative Prescribing Budgets for General Medical Practitioners*, London: HMSO.

Department of Health (1989f) *Working Paper 7. NHS Consultants: Appointments, Contracts and Distinction Awards*, London: HMSO.

Department of Health and Social Security (1972) *Management Arrangements for the Reorganised National Health Service*, London: HMSO.

Department of Health and Social Security (1973) *Report of the Committee on Hospital Complaints Procedure* (chaired by Sir Michael Davies), London: HMSO.

Department of Health and Social Security (1983) *Report of the NHS Management Inquiry* (chaired by Roy Griffiths), London: HMSO.

Department of Health and Social Security/Scottish Home and Health Department/ Welsh Office (1983) *Report on the Operation of Procedure for Independent Review of Complaints involving the Clinical Judgement of Hospital Doctors and Dentists*, London: HMSO.

Derbyshire, R. (1983) 'How Effective is Medical Self-Regulation?', *Law and Human Behavior* 7: 193–202.

Derom, R., Pelfrene, E., Vlietinck, R. and Thiery, M. (1989) 'Organization of Obstetrical Care in Belgium', *Biology of the Neonate* 55: 63–9.

Devlin, H. (1988) 'Professional Audit; Quality Control; Keeping up to Date', *Baillière's Clinical Anesthesiology* 2: 299–324.

Dingwall, R., Fenn, P. and Quam, L. (1991) *Medical Negligence: A Review and Bibliography*, Oxford: Centre for Socio-Legal Studies.

Doherty, E. and Haven, C. (1977) 'Medical Malpractice and Negligence: Socio-demographic Characteristics of Claimants and Non-claimants', *Journal of American Medical Association* 238: 1656–8.

Drucker, P. (1974) *Management: Tasks, Responsibilities, Practices*, London: Heinemann.

Drummond, M. and Morgan, J. (1988) in *Learning From Complaints*, National Association of Health Authorities Members' Information Pamphlet No. 6.

Eckerlund, I. (1986) 'Model Health Care Programmes', *European Newsletter on Quality Assurance* 3: 4.

Eckstein, H. (1958) *The English Health Service*, Cambridge, Mass: Harvard University Press.

Felstiner, W., Abel, R. and Sarat, A. (1980–81) 'The Emergence and Transformation of Disputes: Naming, Blaming, Claiming . . . ', *Law and Society Review* 15: 631–54.

Fenn, P. and Dingwall, R. (1990) 'The Problems of Crown Indemnity', in Gretton, J. (ed.), *Health Care UK 1989*, Birmingham: Policy Journals.

Flatten, G. (1988) 'Qualitätssicherung in der Kassenpraxis', *Ärzteblatt Baden-Württemberg* 26–8.

Florida Governor's Review of the Insurance and Tort Systems (1987) *Preliminary Fact-Finding Report on Medical Malpractice*, Florida: Academic Task Force for Review of the Insurance and Tort Systems.

Forsyth, G. (1966) *Doctors and State Medicine: A Study of the British Health Service*, London: Pitman.

Fox, R. (1980) 'The Evolution of Medical Uncertainty', *Milbank Memorial Fund Quarterly* 58: 1–49.

Freidson, E. (1970) *Profession of Medicine: A Study of the Sociology of Applied Knowledge*, New York: Dodd Mead.

Freidson, E. (1975) *Doctoring Together*, New York: Elsevier.

Freidson, E. (1989) *Medical Work in America: Essays on Health Care*, New Haven: Yale University Press.

Fry, G. (1984) 'The Development of the Thatcher Government's "Grand Strategy" for the Civil Service: A Public Policy Perspective', *Public Administration* 62: 321–35.

Fry, G. (1988) 'The Thatcher Government, the Financial Management Initiative, and the "New Civil Service"', *Public Administration* 66: 1–20.

Fry, G., Flynn, A., Gray, A., Jenkins, W. and Rutherford, B. (1988) 'Symposium on Improving Management in Government', *Public Administration* 66: 429–45.

Galanter, M. (1974) 'Why the "Haves" Come Out Ahead: Speculations on the Limits of Legal Change', *Law and Society Review* 9: 95–160.

Galanter, M. (1975) 'Afterword: Explaining Litigation', *Law and Society Review* 9: 347–68.

Garfinkel, H. (1967) *Studies in Ethnomethodology*, Englewood Cliffs: Prentice-Hall.

Garrett, J. (1986) 'Developing State Audit in Britain', *Public Administration* 64: 421–33.

General Medical Council (1983–89) *Annual Reports*, London: General Medical Council.

General Medical Council (1983) *Professional Conduct and Discipline: Fitness to Practise*, London: General Medical Council.

Gostin, L. (1982) 'Complaints and the National Health Service', *LAG Bulletin* March: 27.

Grad, F. and Marti, N. (1979) *Physicians' Licensure and Discipline*, Dobbs Ferry, NY: Oceana.

Greenhouse, J. (1986) *Praying for Justice: Faith, Order and Community in an American Town*, Ithaca, NY: Cornell University Press.

Griffiths, E.R. (1983) *NHS Management Inquiry*, letter to Secretary of State for Social Services, DHSS, 6 October.

Griffiths, J. (1977) 'The Distribution of Legal Services in the Netherlands', *British Journal of Law and Society* 4: 260–86.

Griggs, E. (1989) *Health Care Quality and the NHS White Paper: An Introduction and Overview*, unpublished mimeo.

Ham, C. and Hunter, D. (1988) *Managing Clinical Activity in the NHS*, London: King's Fund Institute.

Harley, M. (1988) 'Performance Indicators in the Management Process', *Health Service Management Research* 1: 29–42.

Harris, J.E. (1977) 'The Internal Organisation of Hospitals: Some Economic Implications', *Bell Journal of Economics* 8: 467–82.

Harrison, S. (1988) *Managing the NHS: Shifting the Frontier*, London: Chapman and Hall.

Harrison, S., Hunter, D.J., Johnston, I. and Wistow, G. (1989) *Competing for Health: A Commentary on the NHS Review*, Leeds: Nuffield Institute for Health Services Studies.

Harrison, S. and Schultz, R. (1989) 'Clinical Autonomy in the United Kingdom and the United States: Contrasts and Convergences', in Freddi, G. and Björkman, J., *The Comparative Politics of Health Governance*, London: Sage.

Harvard Medical Practice Study (1990) *Patients, Doctors, and Lawyers: Medical Injury, Malpractice Litigation, and Patient Compensation in New York*, New York: Harvard Medical Practice Study.

Haywood, S. and Alaszewski, A. (1980) *Crisis in the Health Service*, London: Croom Helm.

Hirshleifer, J. (1971) 'The Private and Social Value of Information and the Reward to Inventive Activity', *American Economic Review* 61: 561–74.

Hoffenberg, R. (1986) *Clinical Freedom*, London: Nuffield Provincial Hospitals Trust.

Holdsworth, Sir W. (1942) *A History of English Law*, London: Methuen/Sweet and Maxwell.

Hood, C. (1990) 'Beyond the Public Bureaucracy State? Public Administration in the 1990s', extended text of an inaugural lecture delivered on 16 January 1990, London: London School of Economics.

Hughes, D. (1991) 'The Reorganisation of the National Health Service: The Rhetoric and Reality of the Internal Market', *Modern Law Review* 54: 88–103.

Hughes, D. and Dingwall, R. (1990a) 'Sir Henry Maine, Joseph Stalin and the Reorganization of the National Health Service', *Journal of Social Welfare Law* 296–309.

Hughes, D. and Dingwall, R (1990b) 'What's in a Name?', *Health Service Journal* 100, 5229: 1770–1, (29 November).

Hughes, E. (1951) 'Mistakes at Work', *Canadian Journal of Economics and Political Science* 17: 320–7.

Hunting, R. and Neuwith, G. (1962) *Who Sues in New York City? A Study of Automobile Accident Claims*, New York: Columbia University Press.

' Institute of Medicine (1990) *Medicare: A Strategy for Quality Assurance* (2 vols), Washington DC: National Academy Press.

Jacob, J. (1988) *Doctors and Rules: A Sociology of Professional Values*, London: Routledge.

Jacob, J. and Davies, J.V. (1987) *Encyclopaedia of Health Services and Medical Law*, London: Sweet and Maxwell.

Jacquerye, A. (1987) *Introducing Quality Assurance in Nursing*, unpublished mimeo.

Jamous, H. and Peloille, B. (1970) 'Professions or Self-perpetuating Systems? Changes in the French University Hospital System', in Jackson, J.A. (ed.), *Professions and Professionalization*, Cambridge, UK: Cambridge University Press.

Jenkins, L., Beardsley, M., Coles, J., Wickings, I. and Leow, H. (1987) *Use and Validity of NHS Performance Indicators*, Bath: Centre for Analysis of Social Policy in Europe (CASPE).

Johnson, T.J. (1981) *Professions and Power*, London: Macmillan.

Jost, T.S. (1990) *Assuring the Quality of Medical Practice: An International Comparative Study*, London: King's Fund.

Katz, D. (1984) 'Bad Doctors', *Detroit Free Press*, Parts I–IV, 1 April, 3, 6, 8.

King's Fund Institute (1988) *Health Finance: Assessing the Options*, London: King's Fund Institute.

Klazinga, N. (1989) *Results of a Global Inventory about Quality Assurance Activities in the Different Countries of the European Community*, third draft, unpublished mimeo.

Klein, R. (1973) *Complaints against Doctors*, London: Charles Knight.

Klein, R. (1989) *The Politics of the NHS*, 2nd edition, London: Longman.

Klein, R. (1990) 'From Status to Contract: The Transformation of the British Health Profession', paper delivered at the Anglo-American Symposium, University of North Carolina at Chapel Hill, 17–19 May.

Kusserow, R. (1990) *State Medical Boards and Medical Discipline*, Report of the Department of Health and Human Services' Office of Inspector General, Washington, DC: Government Printing Office.

Light, D.W. and Levine, S. (1988) 'The Changing Character of the Medical Profession', *Milbank Quarterly* 66, Supplement 2: 10–32, New York: Cambridge University Press.

Likierman, A. (1982) 'Management Information for Ministers: The MINIS System in the Department of the Environment', *Public Administration* 60: 127–42.

Lord Chancellor's Department (1988) *Report of the Review Body on Civil Justice*, Cmd. 394, London: HMSO.

McNeil, K., Nevin, J., Trubek, D. and Miller, R. (1979) 'Market Discrimination against the Poor and Impact of Consumer Disclosure Laws: The Used Car Industry', *Law and Society Review* 13: 695–720.

March, J. and Olsen, J. (1976) *Ambiguity and Choice in Organizations*, Bergen: Universitetsforlaget.

Martin, S. (1983) *Managing Without Managers*. Beverly Hills: Sage.

Maxwell, R. (1984) 'Quality Assessment in Health', *British Medical Journal* 288: 1470–1.

May, M. and Stengel, D. (1990) *Who Sues Their Doctors? How Patients Handle Medical Grievances*, Madison, WI: Institute for Legal Studies, University of Wisconsin.

Maynard, A. (1988) 'The Public and Private Regulation of Health Care Markets', pp. 133–66 in Sass, H.M. and Massey, R.U. (eds), *Health Care Systems*, Dordrecht: Kluwer.

Miller, F. (1987) 'Clinical Autonomy', *Massachusetts Medicine* January/February: 19–21.

Millman, M. (1977) *The Unkindest Cut: Life in the Backrooms of Medicine*, New York: Wm Morrow.

Ministry of Health (1944) *A National Health Service*, Cmd. 6502, London: HMSO.

Ministry of Health and Social Affairs (1986) *The Assessment of Medical Technology – A Proposal for National Coordination*, Task Force Report (unpublished).

Moore, S. (1973) 'Law and Social Change: The Semi-Autonomous Field as an Appropriate Subject of Study', *Law and Society Review* 7: 719–46.

Nader, L. (1980) 'Alternatives to the American Judicial System', in Nader, L. (ed.), *No Access to Law: Alternatives to the American Judicial System*, New York: Academic Press.

National Association of Quality Assurance (in Health Care)(1988) *Journal and Conference Proceedings*, Peterborough: M.G. Hillson.

National Audit Office (1988) *Quality of Clinical Care in National Health Service Hospitals*, London: HMSO.

National Confidential Enquiry into Perioperative Deaths (1989) *Report*, London: NCEPOD.

NHS Management Executive (1989) *Quality*, Management Directive, 22 June.

Niskanen, W. (1971) *Bureaucracy and Representative Government*, Chicago: Aldine.

O'Brien, J. (1987) 'Providing a Quality Approach to Health Care at the Regional Level: An Idiosyncratic View', in *Creating Quality in the NHS*, Centre for Professional Development, Department of Community Medicine, The Medical School, Manchester.

Ott, S. (1989) *The Organizational Culture Perspective*, Chicago: Dorsey Press.

Paget, M. (1988) *The Unity of Mistakes*, Philadelphia: Temple University Press.

Parsons, T. (1952) *The Social System*, London: Routledge and Kegan Paul.

Pater, J.E. (1981) *The Making of the National Health Service*, London: King Edward's Hospital Fund for London.

Pelling, M. and Webster, C. (1979) 'Medical Practitioners', in Webster, C. (ed.),

Health, Medicine and Mortality in the Sixteenth Century, Cambridge, UK: Cambridge University Press.

Pendleton, D., Schofield, T. and Marinker, M. (1986) *In Pursuit of Quality*, London: Royal College of General Practitioners.

Petchey, R. (1986) 'The Griffiths Reorganisation of the National Health Service: Fowlerism by Stealth?', *Critical Social Policy* 6: 87–101.

Peters, T. and Waterman, R. (1982) *In Search of Excellence*, New York: Harper and Row.

Pine, L., Rosenqvit, L., Rosenthal, M. and Shapiro, F. (1988) 'The Swedish Medical Care Programmes: An Internal Assessment', *Health Policy* 10: 155–76.

Pollitt, C. (1987) 'Capturing Quality? The Quality Issue in British and American Health Policy', *Journal of Public Policy* 7: 71–92.

Pollitt, C., Harrison, S., Hunter, D.J. and Marnoch, G. (1988) 'The Reluctant Managers: Clinicians and Budgets in the NHS', *Financial Accountability and Management* 4: 213–33.

Prescott-Clarke, P., Brooks, T. and Machray, C. (1988) *Focus on Health Care: Surveying the Public in Four Health Districts*, Vol.1, London: Social and Community Planning Research/Royal Institute of Public Administration.

Public Accounts Committee (1980–81) *Financial Control and Accountability in the NHS*, 17th Report HC 255, London: HMSO.

Public Citizen Health Research Group (1990a) *6892 Questionable Doctors Disciplined by State or Federal Government*, Washington, DC: Public Citizen Health Research Group.

Public Citizen Health Research Group (1990b) *Health Letter* April.

Rawlings, R. (1987) *Grievance Procedures and Administrative Justice: A Review of Socio-Legal Research*, London: Economic and Social Research Council.

Rayner, Lord (1984) *The Unfinished Agenda*, Stamp Memorial Lecture.

Reizenstein, P., Blackman, M., Bildt, H., Bavenholm, R., Hasselgran, A-M., Ramgren, O. and Tengmark, B-O. (1987) *Quality Assurance in the Stockholm County Council*, unpublished mimeo.

Robinson, J. (1988) *A Patient Voice at the GMC*, London: Health Rights.

Roger, F. (1988) 'L'Evaluation de la Qualité des Soins', *Acta Clinica Belgica* 43: 219–30.

Rosenberg, C. (1987) *The Care of Strangers: The Rise of America's Hospital System*, New York: Basic Books.

Rosenthal, M. (1987/1988) *Dealing with Medical Malpractice: The British and Swedish Experience*, London/Durham, NC: Tavistock/Duke University Press.

Rosenthal, M. and Fredericks, D. (1985) Unpublished study of State of Michigan Medical Board.

Ross, L. and Littlefield, N. (1978) 'Complaint as a Problem Solving Mechanism', *Law and Society Review* 12: 181–216.

Royal College of General Practitioners (1985a) *What Sort of Doctor? Assessing Quality of Care in General Practice*, London: RCGP.

Royal College of General Practitioners (1985b) *Quality in General Practice*, London: RCGP.

Royal College of Physicians (1990) *Medical Audit: A First Report: What, Why and How?*, London: RCP.

Royal College of Surgeons (1989) *Guidelines to Clinical Audit in Surgical Practice*, London: RCS.

Sachverständigenrat für die Konzertierte Aktion im Gesundheitswesen (1989) *Qualität, Wirkschaftlichkeit und Perspektiven der Gesundheitsversorgung: Vorschläge für die Konzertierte Aktion im Gesundheitswesen: Jahresgutachten 1989.*

Saville, J. (1983) 'The Origins of the Welfare State', in Loney, M., Boswell, D. and Clarke, J. (eds), *Social Policy and Social Welfare*, Milton Keynes: Open University Press.

Schega, W. (1984) 'Qualitätssicherung in der Chirurgie', in *Beitrage zur Gesundheitsökonomie: Qualitätssicherung Ärztlichen Handelns*, Stuttgart: Robert Bosch Stiftung.

Schein, E.H. (1985) *Organizational Culture and Leadership: A Dynamic View*, San Francisco: Jossey Bass.

Schenk, W. (1988) 'Who Should be the Responsible Surgeon in the Surgical Intensive Care Unit?', *Current Surgery* September–October: 361–2.

Schulz, R. and Johnson, A. (1983) *Management of Hospitals*, 2nd edition, New York: McGraw-Hill.

Schwartz, F-W. (1984) 'Praktizierte Qualitätssicherung in der Ambulanten Versorgung der Bundesrepublik Deutschland', in *Beitrage zur Gesundheitsökonomie: Qualitätssicherung Ärztlichen Handelns*, Stuttgart: Robert Bosch Stiftung.

Selbmann, H-K. (1982) 'Approaches Towards Quality Assurance in Medical Care in the Federal Republic of Germany', in Selbmann, H.K. and Überla, K., *Quality Assessment of Medical Care*, Stuttgart: Robert Bosch Stiftung.

Shaw, C. (1986a) *Introducing Quality Assurance*, London: King's Fund Centre.

Shaw, C. (1986b) *Quality Assurance: What the Colleges Are Doing*, London: King's Fund Centre.

Shaw, C. (1987) *Quality Assurance in the NHS: Current Management Approaches*, London: King's Fund Centre.

Shaw, C. (1988) 'Quality Assurance: A New Epidemic', *NAHA News* June: 12.

Shaw, C. (1989), *Medical Audit: A Hospital Handbook*, London: King's Fund Centre.

Smith, R. (1989) 'Profile of the GMC: Discipline (3 parts)', *British Medical Journal* 298: 1502–5, 1569–71, 1632–4.

Social Services Committee (1988–89) *Reforming the National Health Service: The Government's Plans for the Future of the National Health Service*, Eighth Report from the Social Services Committee, session 1988–89, HC 214–111.

SPRI (1986) *Three Years Ahead*, Stockholm: SPRI.

SPRI (1987) *Listen to the Patients: Here Are the Questions*, Stockholm: SPRI.

Stacey, M. (1976) 'The Health Service Consumer: A Sociological Misconception', in Stacey, M. (ed.), *The Sociology of the National Health Service*, Sociological Review Monograph 22, Keele: University of Keele.

State of Michigan, Department of Licensing and Regulation (1990) Private correspondence, May and October.

Steele, E. (1977) 'Two Approaches to Contemporary Dispute Behaviour and Consumer Problems', *Law and Society Review* 11: 667–77.

Strauss, A., Fagerhaugh, S., Suczek, B. and Wiener, C. (1985) *Social Organization of Medical Work*, Chicago and London: University of Chicago Press.

Templeton College (1987) *Templeton Series on District Managers: DGMs and Quality Improvement*, Oxford: Templeton College.

Towell, D. (1987) 'Notes Towards a Strategy for Pursuing Quality in the NHS', in

Creating Quality in the NHS, Centre for Professional Development, Department of Community Medicine, The Medical School, Manchester.

Truelove, A. (1985) 'On Handling Complaints', *Hospital and Health Services Review* September: 229.

US General Accounting Office (GAO) (1987) *Medical Malpractice: Characteristics of Claims Closed in 1984*, Washington, DC: General Accounting Office.

Varlam, C. (1978) 'History of the General Medical Council', PhD thesis, Department of Sociology and Social Policy, Bedford College, University of London.

Vidmar, N. (1981) 'Justice Motives and Other Psychological Factors in the Development and Resolution of Disputes', in Lerner, M. and Lerner, S. (eds), *The Justice Motive in Social Behavior: Adapting to Times of Scarcity and Change*, New York: Plenum Press.

Vouri, H. (1982) *Quality Assurance of Health Services*, Copenhagen: World Health Organization.

Vouri, H. (1989) 'Scandinavian Model Health Care Programs – A Cousin of Quality Assurance', *International Journal of Quality Assurance* 22–6.

Watkin, B. (1978) *The National Health Service: The First Phase*, London: George Allen and Unwin.

Webster, C. (1988) *The Health Services since the War. Volume 1, Problems of Health Care: The National Health Service before 1957*, London: HMSO.

Wheeler, S., Cartwright, B., Kagan, R. and Friedman, L. (1987) 'Do the "Haves" Come Out ahead? Winning and Losing in State Supreme Courts, 1870–1970', *Law and Society Review* 21: 403–45.

World Health Organization (1988) *World Health Statistics Annual – 1988*, Geneva: World Health Organization.

World Health Organization, Regional Office for Europe (1985) *Targets for Health for All*, Copenhagen: World Health Organization.

Index